Crushing Your Fear

Michael Power

Crushing Your Fear, published September, 2022

Editorial and proofreading services: Highline Editorial, New York, NY; Katie Barger
Interior layout and cover design: Howard Johnson
Photo Credits: Cover photo by 7 Seconds Media, *7secondsmedia.us*

SDP Publishing

Published by SDP Publishing, an imprint of SDP Publishing Solutions, LLC.

ISBN-13 (print): 979-8-9856475-8-7
ISBN-13 (ebook): 979-8-9856475-9-4

Library of Congress Control Number: 2022909025

Printed in the United States of America

TABLE OF CONTENTS

FOREWORD

Our deepest fear is not that we are inadequate. Our deepest fear is that we are powerful beyond measure. It is our light, not our darkness, that most frightens us. We ask ourselves, Who am I to be brilliant, gorgeous, talented, fabulous? Actually, who are you not to be? You are a child of God. Your playing small does not serve the world. There is nothing enlightened about shrinking so that other people won't feel insecure around you. We are all meant to shine, as children do. We were born to make manifest the glory of God that is within us. It is not just in some of us; it is in everyone, and as we let our own light shine, we unconsciously give other people permission to do the same. As we are liberated from our own fear, our presence automatically liberates others.

—**Marianne Williamson**, *A Return to Love: Reflections on the Principles of "A Course in Miracles"*

As a bestselling author, speaker, leadership mentor, and coach, I work with entrepreneurs and executives who are extremely successful externally, yet are still craving greater fulfillment and impact. They can feel a wealth of untapped power and potential calling them to step into a higher purpose and legacy, knowing they're capable of more. Despite all the success, they're falling short of the freedom and fulfillment, elevated focus and productivity, and financial abundance they're capable of having, which fuels their self-doubt and sabotage cycles. These are the people to whom I wrote my bestselling book, Be a Boss & Fire That Bitch: Quiet Your Inner Critic & Finally Believe You're GOOD ENOUGH, and the people I surround myself with daily in the InFLOWential Leadership Mastermind.

With over twenty years of leadership experience, from leading missions on the front lines of Iraq 2003 to a corporate career, to starting, building, struggling, failing, and scaling multiple businesses, I've seen all aspects of the leadership spectrum. Each one taught me that leadership and success are an inside job and allows me to empower my clients to tap into effortless success and influential leadership by unlocking their full gifts and potential through the deepest inner work.

However, that's not where I started. My rock-bottom moment was only seven years ago at the time I'm writing this foreword. That extreme low came out of the fact that I was functioning from a place of fear in almost every aspect of my life. The root fear was that I was not enough. So, I always wore a mask of who I thought I should be to avoid rejection or judgment, which ended up being a futile endeavor. I'd never learned how to love myself, fill my own cup, or have a healthy toolkit for handling my emotions, like fear, in a constructive way. At that time, I was simply surviving, not thriving or living at all.

Learning how to make friends with my fear and understand it for what it really is has been a game-changer, personally and professionally. It's what has allowed me to transform inside and out to become the leader I'm called to be in the world, living and leading with my purpose to be of service to others' growth and transformation. However, that wouldn't have happened if I wasn't willing to lean in, get honest with myself, and uncover where the fear came from and what it was telling me. That is exactly what you'll learn from reading this book; how to transform your fear into fuel for change and impact.

Over the years, I've met thousands of coaches, experts, and 'gurus' in the personal and professional development space. Yet, very few actually embodied the energy and practice of what they taught. However, Michael is different. I've watched him lean into his own fear to understand and transmute it to fuel his passion and purpose, like writing this book and speaking on stage. Having walked this path himself and leading by example, he's helping people like you transform your understanding of fear and use it to reach your goals. True freedom comes from turning your fear into passion and purpose! The key is being willing to get honest with yourself about who you are and who you desire to be.

The most powerful aspect of the book you're about to read is, by following the process Michael lays out for you, you'll be able to understand and quickly work through the fear we experience when making changes. Anytime we are called to be and do better, it can trigger the old stories and patterns, fueling the fear that can keep us stuck. He breaks down, step-by-step, the process of not only identifying how the fear is showing up today but also where it came from so you can take your power back from it and become the best you. By the end of this book, not only will you understand your fear, but you'll also have the tools to funnel that emotion into creating the life you desire.

Now it's time to lean in and get honest!

Stacy Raske
Bestselling Author, Speaker
CEO, InFLOWential Leadership Mastermind
Apex Executive Coach
www.stacyraske.com

Introduction

Why am I writing this book?

I see fear as a prevalent force in society that not many people talk about. We talk about circumstances that happen to us in the past and how to deal with negative situations in the present, but we don't talk about the root of these actions and thoughts: fear.

Fear is instilled in us through society. "I don't want to fail that test." *Fear.* "I don't want the neighbors to think less of us." *Fear.* "I don't want to die, so I'd better tell my doctor to prescribe me that medication." *Fear.*

The list is endless, as is the constant stimulus that comes our way through the regular media, social media, and "conforming to society's norms."

My life has had its ups and downs, and certainly, fear was a part of it. I had low self-esteem as a kid, and I was bullied. I have been married and divorced twice. I built a beautiful home and had a family of my own, but I lost it all because of the challenges of starting and maintaining a business (that crashed and burned too).

My rock bottom came when I was on my air mattress in my office in a strip mall with stress-induced eczema, no money, no family, no business, and huge financial pressure. I had two choices: crawl into a corner and accept that life was over, or get my mind and body straight and move forward. I chose the latter.

I started a daily routine of meditation and gym workouts. I signed up for a marathon and started reading and listening to books and podcasts. I joined men's help and entrepreneurial groups to surround myself with strong people. I knew by then that I wanted to write a book about fear, but when I began to write, I realized I needed more information from others who have gone through it and come out successfully on the other side. I started the "Crushing Your Fear" podcast to interview a few wise individuals in my men's group. Then, I reached out to others who agreed to come onto the show and share their wisdom. Now, it seems like everyone wants to come on the show and share!

And I find myself asking these questions: Have I been through a lot of fear-fueled times? Yes. Have I learned (sometimes the hard way) to get through them? Yes. Do I think I can help others with what I have learned and what I continue to learn? Yes. I developed a burning desire to expand beyond my podcast and write a book that people can use as a tool to help them analyze and handle fear.

I have learned a great deal from many different sources and a variety of talented authors. I have done my best to properly cite and quote from these sources. There is a references section that can also be considered recommended reading. These publications have helped me tremendously, and I hope they help you. My goal in writing this book is to compile and present to the reader a well-rounded and well-summarized book surrounding the topic of overcoming fear.

LINKS TO CRUSHING YOUR FEAR

Throughout this book, I have referenced my podcast and other resources that provide the tools that you need to handle YOUR fears. Here is a link to the website where you can find links to the podcast as well as free resources and sign up for a BONUS companion course to the book:

https://www.crushingyourfear.com/

You can also access these resources by pointing your camera on your smartphone here:

Follow and DM me on
Instagram @therealmichaelpower

https://www.instagram.com/therealmichaelpower/

Join our Facebook Community to connect with like-minded individuals and get the support you need

https://www.facebook.com/crushingyourfear

So, here I go with my first book: *Crushing Your Fear.*

—Michael Power, 2022

1

Fear 101

"Obstacles are like wild animals. They are cowards but they will bluff you if they can. If they see you are afraid of them ... they are liable to spring upon you; but if you look them squarely in the eye, they will slink out of sight."

—**Orison Swett Marden**

Fear is primitive in nature. It is inherent in us as a key trigger emotion, which results in a "fight or flight" response. According to research published by Harvard Medical School, the "combination of reactions to stress is also known as the 'fight-or-flight' response because it evolved as a survival mechanism, enabling people and other mammals to react quickly to life-threatening situations."[1]

If you think of a primitive time when cavemen and large, unruly animals roamed the planet, you will understand. Humans were considered food to a saber-toothed tiger, so they needed the emotion of fear to survive in difficult situations. Humans, of course, have advanced brain capacity and have been able to survive over the millennia, but fear was an essential emotion that helped them survive.

The problem arises when humans *perceive* some event—whether present or future—as a threat when it may not be a threat at all. The mind is very complex and can create many different scenarios and outcomes, which can then trigger reactions within the body like an increased heart rate, shortness of breath, and elevated blood pressure. In times of actual danger, such as being in the path of a speeding bus, these shifts from the body's normal state can save your life. However, a constant, recurring loop of these changes in the body can have detrimental, life-changing effects.

The response to stress begins in our brain. If we perceive some type of danger, whether real or not, the amygdala (an almond-shaped mass in our brains that is involved with experiencing emotions) sends a signal to the hypothalamus (the "command center" of the body), which then communicates to the rest of the body through the nervous system to gather the energy to fight or flee.

Next, the sympathetic nervous system kicks into gear and triggers the "fight-or-flight" response. Adrenaline is pumped into the bloodstream, which elevates the heart rate and sends blood to muscles and other organs. The body's blood pressure goes up and breathing becomes rapid. The extra oxygen that's produced is sent to the brain, which increases alertness. Our senses (sight, hearing, etc.) become elevated.

The adrenaline also signals the body to release more blood sugar and fat, which floods the bloodstream and supplies increased energy to all parts of the body.

All of this happens so rapidly that we aren't aware that it's happening. Our bodies react accordingly (i.e., jumping out of the path of an oncoming bus or fleeing into a cave to get away from that tiger), but the brain is not done yet! More hormones and chemicals are released into the body to keep us on high alert until the danger is over. Once the threat passes, the para-sympathetic nervous system slows the body's response to its normal state.

Issues arise when individuals stay in a constant state of increased alert, which is mostly caused by fear. This constant state leads to health problems like damaged arteries, and it can raise the risk of heart attacks and strokes. It also causes increased hunger as the body tries to replenish energy stored before the triggered response, but this can lead to a buildup of fat tissue and weight gain. As a result, experiencing fear is not just detrimental to the mind, it is detrimental to the body as well.

In "A Brief History of Anxiety & Fear," Garrett Ray Harriman explains that the ancient Greek philosophers examined fear and came up with some pretty impressive thoughts that we can apply in modern-day society. They viewed the mind and body as intimately connected, as many individuals do today.[2]

Aristotle believed fear and confidence were opposites, just as other things could be defined by their opposing characteristics, such as wet and dry, and hot and cold. Aristotle was on the right path, but he did not support the concept of "fearlessness." He considered it crazy not to fear the gods and the influence they had on the environment. He also considered the heart as the center of the body, with an angry person's blood radiating away from the heart and causing angry behaviors and thoughts. In contrast, the blood in a fear-stricken person was drawn toward the heart, making the body cold and causing trembling and sweating.[3]

Another Greek philosopher, Galen, agreed with Aristotle's idea of "balance" to control thoughts and feelings. He believed that for an individual to live a fulfilling inner and outer life, an ideal balance of opposites must be the goal. In cases of extreme fear, the balance was so disrupted that some people suffered fears of imaginary things. As for the physical symptoms, he believed imbalance also played a part: "... he [Galen] felt trembling was caused by bearing too heavy of an emotional burden."[4]

The philosopher Epicurious believed that the mind, body, and soul were composed of tiny particles (atoms), and the misalignment of these atoms in the body and soul—caused by fearful thoughts—led to imbalance and pain. He concluded that it was

"... best to avoid and predict fear, not overcome it through virtuous acts."[5]

Through the medieval period and the Renaissance, fear was also believed to cause imbalances and interactions of atoms in the mind, soul, and body. Doctors and thinkers in this period believed that a person's well-being was determined by the harmony of their bodily fluids, also known as the four "humours." These humours were: "...black bile (*melancholic,* sad or depressed), yellow/red bile (*choleric,* easily angered or disturbed) blood (*sanguine*, optimistic and coura-geous), and phlegm (*phlegmatic*, calm and patient)."[6]

Through the humoric approach, an individual was diagnosed as fearful based on their temperament, which was a result of their humoric configuration. Doctors prescribed changes in environment and diet to restore balance and reduce fear and its effects on the mind and body.[7]

Now that we have a better understanding of the historical theories on fear and its effects on the mind and body, let's look at mass events that have caused fear in people. Events such as plagues and terrorist attacks have caused individuals to react in different ways and, at times, create a new "norm."

At the time of writing this book, COVID-19 is the headline story and has instilled great fear in many people. But this is definitely not the first time in history that plagues and related casualties have affected the minds of the masses. The black plague pandemic, which lasted from 1346 to 1350, claimed up to 100 million lives and is still a recognizable term when the topic of widespread disease arises. The Spanish flu pandemic of 1918 is referenced when health profes-sionals discuss the current environment. Now, with 24-hour news, there is a constant fear of injury or death related to mass events (such as COVID-19), and this can contribute to an individual's mental breakdown.

In "Fears, Outbreaks, and Pandemics: Lessons Learned," Nidal Moukaddam discusses the fact that pre-existing anxiety and depressive disorders can amplify this fear. Individuals can even relapse into destructive substance abuse to deal with the increased stress. Fear can also cause skin disorders in certain people. This happened to me when fear of losing everything caused a flare-up of severe eczema on my arms, legs, and back. Through a mix of facing my fears, meditation, and changing my eating habits, I was able to reverse that condition, but it wasn't easy.[8]

In the late 1940s—after World War II—there was a steady increase in fear about the threat presented by Communists in the U.S. because of an alleged conspiracy to destroy America. This fear peaked in the early 1950s and remained steady for another decade.

The 1995 Oklahoma City bombing that resulted in 168 deaths was the second-most destructive terrorist act ever in the U.S. and one of the worst in American history.[9] This heinous act created a deep primitive fear that terrorism could happen again anywhere on American soil.

After the terrorist attacks of Sept. 11, 2001, American fears of terrorism spiked sharply. In the following weeks and months, more than 70 percent of Americans believed that another terrorist attack was likely and that more Americans would be killed. This fueled a specific fear of Islamist terrorism, which was viewed as an international conspiracy with dormant "cells" waiting to attack at a moment's notice.[10]

In the following chapters, we will address different situations in which fear arises, the triggers for those fears, and what you can do to handle them as they arise.

Take a moment to look back at your life. Think about times when you felt fear and what you did to deal with it. Look at the source that triggered those fears. Was it a parent who instilled the "fear of God" into you with one sentence that has remained with you? Was it a newscast that reported a sharp increased risk in your safety due to events happening thousands of miles away? Was it your decision not to take that chance on a career change because of your uncle's advice (even though he had zero experience in that area)?

What happens to your body when random, (sometimes) baseless thoughts cause the trigger of emotions that lead to negative chain reactions that cause chaos in your mind, body, and soul? The long-term effects on your well-being can be devastating—effects that include a deterioration of your mental and physical fortitude as well as creating a negative impact on the lives of others. You will also miss out on opportunities to enrich your life by avoiding experiences due to fear.

I ask you to take all of the above and really think about the events and reactions you had when you experienced fear. You may also be currently in a state of fear due to a certain situation or set of circumstances. What is causing that fear? Is it a real, tangible threat? Or is it fabricated and being blown out of proportion, i.e., not in alignment with reality? Are you relying on the beliefs of another individual, or are you taking your news correspondent's views as truth without verifying through other sources? Are you making conclusions on what will happen if you venture into some new business or relationship based on what you have experienced in the past, or are you looking at the potential to do something great that will affect many people?

When I started building out my brewery, we had a lot of plumbers, electricians, excavators, and other workers/machinery involved. One time, I faced fear when a plumber recommended a financing company to help me with his costs. I was relying on these funds to pay him, but when I went to the financing company to discuss a loan, I was told that they only did residential loans, not commercial. The brewery work was obviously commercial.

When I communicated this to the plumber, he said it wasn't his problem and he needed more money as soon as possible for previous work done or he wouldn't finish the minor work necessary. If he didn't complete what he'd started, I couldn't satisfy the city inspector, which meant I wouldn't be able to open. Up to that date, I had invested tens of thousands of dollars to get the brewery built out. My mind started to race, and the fear of losing *everything* set in.

I resolved that giving up wasn't an option. I searched for and found another plumber to do the minor tasks, and we satisfied the city inspector. We opened a month later, and I found another loan source to pay off the first plumber.

2

Fear of Family

"We can easily forgive a child who is afraid of the dark; the real tragedy of life is when men are afraid of the light." —Plato

There are "healthy" families where Mom and Dad support and encourage their children to follow their dreams. Love and understanding are pervasive within these families. Children are taught how to think for themselves and conquer the challenges they face. These types of families act as a single unit and ride out the peaks and valleys of life together.

However, for a large number of families, a lot of fear exists within the family unit itself, so much so that it could be considered to be the source of an epidemic. Childhood anxiety and depression are on the rise, and according to the National Institute of Mental Health, an estimated 40 million Americans suffer from some type of anxiety disorder. We have to ask ourselves: What is the source of this fear? Why is it running rampant within our families?

A common belief is that we, as parents, acquired fears from *our* parents and are passing them to our children. Our parents shaped us by what they believed to be true and taught us how to handle (or mishandle) the experiences we face. We must face any fears that were instilled into us and deal with them *before* we pass them to our kids. This is critical to developing healthy, confident children. If we ignore our own fears, the transmission of these fears to our children will be inevitable.

The advancement of smartphones and access to social media has also had a negative impact on families. It has essentially driven family members into isolation by giving them excuses to stay indoors and avoid interaction with other individuals and with nature. This creates a false sense of safety by providing opportunities to avoid fear. The media does not help this situation by broadcasting doom and gloom on a 24-hour cycle. (Note: We will address the media in another chapter.)

In 2019, I was driving for Uber in Boston—you do what you need to do to support your family—and I picked up a young man in his early twenties near Boston University. We started a conversation, and I asked him, "What are you studying at BU?"

He responded that he was in a program to become a pharmacist.

"Wow, that's interesting!" I said. "How do you like it?"

"I hate it," he replied.

Taken aback, I asked, "Then why are you studying to be a pharmacist?"

"Because my aunt and uncle are pharmacists, and they told me it would be good for me."

He was clearly unhappy about his decision to pursue a career in which he found no joy.

This sheltered "Listen, we know what's best for you" scenario is very common. Families have opinions. They know what's "best for you." Most of the time, it comes from a place of love because your family cares about you and doesn't want to see you hurt or struggle. You need some guidance on how to proceed in life, so you listen to what they have to say.

But what happens when we ignore our inner voice telling us to take Path A when the family tells us to take Path B?

Imagine a conversation with your family. Your dad says, "Don't risk *everything*." Your mom backs up your dad. "Be safe," she says. Then, Dad hits hard with the classic comment: "Why don't you get a *real* job and stop fooling around?"

Their advice confuses us and creates fear. It makes us question our own judgment. Is their idea the right way? Are we being irresponsible for wanting something else for our lives?

Let's explore further. The following example is based on the "perfect" family. (I'll discuss families as incubators of fear later.)

When we come into this world, family is the first experience we have. They wrap us in blankets, take us to a warm place, and make sure we are safe as we grow. We are attached to them. There are no other people we trust more. We take in a lot of information, and if we're confused, we ask them for the answer. Everything is great because family is there to take care of us.

Then, we start school. We encounter a lot of strangers, and a teacher begins to tell us what to do and how to act. We make friends who have been molded by the impressions of their own families. There are a lot of new and scary things. But we always get to go home to the comfort of our own families.

We progress through school, following the path laid out for us by our teachers and parents. Then, we get to the crossroads: Should I go to college? We start rationalizing and debating with ourselves: What am I interested in? I really like art and I draw well. Should I search for a program that develops that skill? This uncertainty—this fear—leads us to ask for advice from our families.

Dad counsels with: "Well, Son, your grandfather and I are doctors, and you should study medicine too. Don't fool around. You'll have your own family one day, and you'll need to take care of them."

Your Uncle Ted jumps in: "I'm a lawyer and have done well. Go into law. That's your calling! Why do you want to waste time being a starving artist? Wake up!"

You submit to their advice and toss aside your desire to be an artist. You commit to a *massive* student loan to get you through the "family-endorsed" college program. You go through the motions in classes you're not interested in, but you tell yourself that in four years, you'll be set with a great job and a huge salary. Graduation day arrives and your family is proud. You've even accepted a job offer at a company with a salary that makes your friends envious.

But when you start this new career, you quickly realize that you hate it. You question what you're doing and wish that you were drawing and creating rather than sitting in a tiny office cube going through the motions. You have a massive loan to pay off, so you feel stuck. You think you have to ride it out and can only hope things will get better.

As time goes on, you find a partner, get married, and have kids because that is what your mom and dad did. You start planning to buy a better house, but that means a mortgage and more debt. You begin to wonder how you got into this situation. You're not happy, but you can't change careers because it's a steady income, and you have responsibilities.

This is the scenario that plays out over and over again in our society. The stress it puts on individuals and families is huge. It's arguably one of the contributing factors to the high divorce rate: a partner gets frustrated in a job they hate and resents the fact that they have to stay in that job to support the family. This frustration leads to distancing from their current partner, infidelity, and substance abuse, to name a few. All because Uncle Ted, the lawyer said, "Wake Up!"

Fear can also manifest as the fear of one day not having your *own* family. Here's a scenario: Jill seeks out her ideal mate. But what criteria does she use? When she asks family members for advice, they usually say she should look for someone with a "good job who will take care of you and your family." With this prerequisite in mind, Jill seeks out men based on the size of their wallets rather than the size of their hearts.

Time passes, and Jill's prospects become sparse. Her "biological clock" enters the picture, and fear sets in. What if she doesn't find anyone? What if she doesn't have kids? Will she die alone? The advice of finding a man with a good job as the main criteria didn't work, and her fear causes her to settle for someone she might not otherwise have chosen.

Men aren't exempt from wanting families either. Jack is seeking his "ideal" mate but hasn't found anyone who meets his criteria. He's getting older, and he begins to question whether he should consider an arranged marriage, which is how his parents met and wed. His siblings now all have families and kids of their own too. They have stable jobs and money put away. Would it be so wrong to consider the path of his parents? Maybe one of his siblings could set him up with someone they know.

And that's exactly what happens. A friend of Jack's sister sets Jack up with her cousin. Jack isn't all that impressed—she seems kind of needy—but nobody's perfect, right? Plus, he knows from his sister that she's from a good family. Jack thinks he should move forward with the relationship.

Like Jill, Jack's biological clock (yes, men have them too!) and the fear that he might not have a family sends him into a less-than-ideal marriage. What are the chances of either of these people's lives being drama-free going forward? It doesn't look great, and it all came about because of fear.

How to Deal with Fear in Your Family
Follow Your Passion and Do What You Want

As children, we are fearless. When it snowed, I always took my sled to the highest hill I could find and pointed it straight down that hill. Think about all the exciting careers we had in mind when we were kids. We wanted to be astronauts or race car drivers or artists. But as we get older, we're told to stop dreaming and get real. We're lectured that we need to go to school and get straight As or study a specific subject in college so that our futures are secure after graduation. We're told to find that "special someone" and get married and have kids. Our dreams of being astronauts fade, and we conform to others' expectations.

Everyone (especially family members) has their opinion on what is best for you, and it's easy to take the safe route and do what they say. But to do something great—to make a difference in the world—requires you to have the courage to say, "No, I'm following *my* dream!"

The good news is that it's never too late to rekindle whatever passion you gave up. Maybe you missed the window to work for NASA, but that doesn't mean you can't get into another industry you dreamed about. Start a podcast and interview people at NASA. Do *anything* to get you closer to what you really want to do.

Take me, for example. I started out as an auditor, but I quickly discovered that my job wasn't fulfilling for me. It didn't give me opportunities to help others in any significant way. I see people lost and afraid daily. This motivated me to take the fear that I experienced, start a podcast, and speak to crowds. Now, I've even written this book.

It's never too late to catch that dream.

Stand Up to Your Extended Family

Say you actually do immerse yourself into learning all you can about NASA, and you get more comments from uncles, aunts, and grandparents. Someone says, "He's going through a mid-life crisis," or "Stop fooling around and get real."

What you need to understand is that most of the time, people have a pre-set way of living. What I mean by that is this: everything seems rosy on the outside. They take pictures with their spouses and families and post them on social media to get "likes." But that doesn't mean everything is great on the inside.

Understand that when people criticize you, it's often because they failed at achieving the very thing you are going for. They don't want to see you succeed because it would just amplify their failure to follow their own dreams. Your success might remind them of their failures. It might bring up negative past experiences and current unfavorable situations that they have not dealt with.

One common piece of advice that I get from guests on my "Crushing Your Fear" podcast is to look your critics in the eyes and tell them you'd like to be around them, but if their criticism continues, you'll need to distance yourself or cut them off completely.

Ryan Michler, founder of Order of Man, was a podcast guest (episode three) with similar advice. He said, "Until the other person pays my bills and takes care of my family, then it's not a matter of what those people think."

The advice might be harsh, but it's part of your journey to overcome fear and live a great life. Surround yourself with people who will build you up, not tear you down. Be strong!

Stand Up to Your Immediate Family

Look at issues you haven't dealt with since childhood. Is it that one sentence that your mom said to you that reverberates inside your head: "Stop dreaming and get a real job"? Do you really want to pass that line of thinking down to your kids? Do you want to be critical of them and instill in them a toxic level of fear? Before you give "sound" advice to your son about wanting to be a race car driver, take a moment and think back to when you were his age. What is it that you would have wanted to hear? Did you hope for encouragement? Were you dying to hear your dad tell you that you were brave for wanting to do something outside of the box? Were you devastated when he, instead, took a flame thrower to your dreams? If you choose to go the flame-thrower route, what kind of an impact do you think that might have on your son?

Take a good look at your family and your interactions with each other. Do you spend quality time together, or are you together in your own "silos"? (Being in a "silo" means everyone is in a room together, but no one is interacting. Instead, everyone is playing games or checking social media on their smartphones.) Having true quality time means—for example—playing a board game or going for a walk together.

In addition, communication with family members is key. You need the kids to feel comfortable coming to you to share any fears they have, and your job is to instill the confidence they need to overcome those fears. Listen to them and understand what is bothering them so you can help them on their journey. (I would also suggest taking their phones away and encouraging them to have friends and get outside!)

3

Fear of Failure

"Ever Tried. Ever Failed. No Matter. Try Again.
Fail Again. Fail Better."   **—Samuel Beckett**

Former extreme skier Kristen Ulmer was a guest on episode nine of my Crushing Your Fear podcast: "Make Fear Your Friend." She said, "Fear does not hold you back; it's your *reaction* to fear that holds you back."

The fear of failure. This one is *huge* and arguably the number one reason we decide not to act on our ideas. (It's right up there with "What will *other* people think?")

How many people have said, "I won't try it because I'll fail?"

I believe everyone has said this to themselves at one point or another in their lives. "What if I fail? I'll get hurt, I'll hurt other people, or I'll create a mess. Everyone will mock and ridicule me and say, 'I told you so!'"

Here is an example of fear controlling a big decision: Jill became a stay-at-home mom while her husband supported the family. She loves her family, but she wonders if there might be more she can do with her life. She asks herself, "Is this it?" She's always enjoyed making necklaces for friends, and she can't help but wonder if she could turn it into a lucrative business. She brainstorms about starting a small, home-based business, and she begins to get excited. She could use the income to help support her family. She begins to research loans so that she can buy equipment and hire a few people to help.

Then the fear creeps in. She rationalizes that her friends like these necklaces, but what if no one else likes them? She'll have no sales and a loan to pay back. She'll also have to lay off her employees. That will put her family and all their families in a bad place. She decides not to move forward with her business idea.

Here is another example: Jack has a great career as a corporate attorney, but every day is the same. He wakes up, drives to work, and sits in meetings. His mind wanders while his colleagues talk, and he daydreams about the past. He thinks back to his time on his college golf team, especially the year they made it to the NCAA finals. "What happened?" he'll think to himself. "Why didn't I follow my dream? I started playing when I was ten years old. I still play every Sunday, and I'm so good that everyone mistakes me for the 'pro' of the course. I really should ditch my day job and go for it. I know I can play with the best of them."

Here comes the fear. "What happens if I'm not that good? I would have left a great-paying job that supports my family to chase an unattainable dream. What am I thinking?"

Imagine all the things that weren't invented that could have made the world a better place, such as finding a cure for a disease. What about the ideas that weren't made into real businesses? Businesses that could have created jobs and wealth for their founders? Think about all the relationships that could have brought two people together.

In many cases, we don't take action to follow through on an idea because of "paralysis by analysis." This is when we have a wonderful idea, but fear steps in and causes us to focus on every possible scenario and every single element of the business that must be "perfect" before we act. The end result is that we usually overwhelm ourselves with "what if" scenarios, and we never follow through with our idea.

You may recall from the previous chapter that Uncle Ted is a pretty good attorney. He has a big client base and is well respected in the community. He has always toyed with the idea of writing a book and being a guest expert in the news to discuss current legal trends in a way the masses can understand.

"I'll get started on writing that book," Ted says to himself. "But I should take a college course in literature first. How am I supposed to write a book when I know nothing about how to do it?"

Two years after he completes that course, Ted still hasn't written his book. Now, he says, "I should take another course in communications to learn about public speaking. I don't want to stand in front of a crowd or be on TV and make a fool of myself."

He completes that course, but a few more years

go by. Ted evaluates where he is in reaching his goals. "I finished my courses, but I have zero experience in writing a book or in public speaking. I have to think about the way forward."

But Ted allows fear to creep into his decision-making and sinks the metaphorical boat. "What happens if I write the book and no one buys it? What happens if I'm on a panel of 'experts' and I can't answer the questions thrown at me? That won't look good to my clients. I'd better scrap the idea altogether. What was I thinking?"

Four years of courses, four years of planning, four years of analysis. But Ted still has no book or speaking engagements. Was that wasted time, money, and energy? YES!

There is a medical term for the fear of failure: atychiphobia (pronounced at-i-kuh-foh-bee-uh). It is an irrational and persistent fear of failing, and if you're a perfectionist (like Uncle Ted), you likely deal with atychiphobia on a semi-regular basis. According to Healthline's article, "What is Atychiphobia and How Can You Manage Fear of Failure?" "Phobias like atychiphobia can be so extreme that they completely paralyze you, making it difficult to carry on with your tasks at home, school, or work." You may even experience some physical symptoms, like difficulty breathing and digestive distress, or you might have emotional symptoms, like an intense feeling of panic or anxiety and an overwhelming need to escape the situation that produces the fear.[11]

You may be more likely to develop atychiphobia if "… you have past experiences where you've failed, especially if the experiences were traumatic or had important consequences, like missing out on an important job."[12]

Failing a test or ending a relationship can also generate trauma and contribute to reluctance to try again. So, in the end, you may miss out on important opportunities in your life, both professionally and personally. You may not take that great job because you didn't think you could handle it, or you never asked that attractive woman out who would have made an amazing partner.[13]

We should also examine our environment to determine the amount of peer pressure that might be present. As a broad example, how does it make us feel when we watch TV, participate in social media, or read magazines that show bikini models and guys with six-pack abs running along a beach with their kids? These glossy images set us up for failure if we don't look like that but feel we should. Peer pressure is all around us, and it makes us feel like we have to act *now* to change ourselves, to fix something that's supposedly wrong with us, so we don't become a failure.

As children, we gravitate into groups of friends that set standards, and anyone who does not conform to those standards is labeled a loser and a failure. If we don't want to be shunned by the group, we succumb to the peer pressure. But by doing that, we give in to the fear of being kicked out of the group.

Another major area where fear of failure always crops up is in relationships. We find ourselves attracted to someone, but fear of rejection stops us from doing anything about it.

Before Jack found his wife, he met many women whom he wanted to ask out on a date. Jack was out one night at a bar with a few friends and saw a woman who worked as a consultant at his company and was in one of his meetings last week.

"Wow, she's awesome," Jack thought to himself. "Great career, powerful woman, and she is stunningly beautiful! I should ask her to dinner."

But the fear of failure intervened.

"Why would she want to be associated with me?" he asks himself. "If she says no, I'll look like a loser in front of my friends. Who am I kidding? She'll never go for me."

How to Deal with Fear of Failure

Acknowledge Your Strengths and Make Your Dream a Reality

Everyone has something they are good at or some idea that can solve a problem in society. Sadly, these strengths and ideas become lost and buried as fear takes over.

If you have a strength or a solid idea, then it's your duty to explore what you can do to make something come from it. Any successful person will tell you of their multiple failures before they hit that one thing that propelled them forward. If you have an idea or a skill that you always wanted to move forward on, then do it!

Thoughts are only thoughts, and we can talk and think all we like. Until we execute and take action on those ideas, they are meaningless. Think of all the people you can help with your new product or program. Think of the income you can generate for your family and the education you can help your kids attain. Think of the possible changes you could bring to your family tree!

You need to get out there and figure out how you will make your idea become reality. You might get rejected for a loan ten times before you get a "yes." But that's okay!

You will need to come up with a business plan, and most likely, a majority of that plan won't go the way you intended. Does that mean it's a failure? No. Each unexpected twist can bring valuable knowledge that allows you to pivot and drive forward in another direction.

Keep testing and be fearless, no matter what anyone else says or thinks. Remember—and this comes from personal experience—if you start getting criticism from others, you are probably on the right track, so keep going!

Overcome Paralysis by Analysis

Many people resolve to create or accomplish something, but they put off completing it because they need "this" or "that" to happen first. They say that they need to save a certain amount of money, or they need to graduate before they can be successful. However, the truth is that you will never have the perfect conditions to try anything, and if you procrastinate, you will inevitably not act on your idea.

The best time to act is now. If you have an idea, and you think it will be great, do it! Don't be paralyzed by "What happens if it doesn't work out?" or "I need more information before I try it." All of these are cop-outs. You won't know if it will work until you test, test, test. Put a well-thought-out business plan together and get the right people involved. Odds are, you will need to revise the business plan and move forward in another direction. Stop the analysis and get it done!

Ask That Girl Out

We see and are attracted to beautiful and talented people, but we ask ourselves: "Why would they want me?"

As a result of this fear, you hesitate to take the first step, rationalizing that the girl won't say yes if you ask her out. How can you rationalize an outcome before you even try? My honest opinion: just go for it and ask her out. If she says yes, good job! If she says no, well, guess what? You're in the same place as you were before you went for it. Your friends might mock you, but there's a simple solution: make new friends. If they don't support you, they're a waste of your time.

Don't Let Past Failures Keep You from Future Victories

Whenever someone fails at something and contemplates trying it again, they're always hindered by the previous failure, and it's used as an excuse not to move forward. This is a big mistake. Why? Because we need to fail. Failure helps us learn what not to do again. I always tell people to fail fast and often, so you know what doesn't work, and you can get to what does work much sooner.

According to the article, "How to Overcome Your Fear of Failure," in *Harvard Business Review*, "It's when you feel comfortable that you should be fearful, because it's a sign that you're not stepping far enough out of your comfort zone to take steps that will help you rise and thrive."[14]

When working toward a goal, make a list of what things you think will go wrong and do them anyway. You need to step into that uncomfortable space to grow and attain what you want.

Take comfort in the thought that you *will* fail, but failing is part of the journey to success.

Fail better!

4

Fear in the Workplace

"Too many people are thinking of security instead of opportunity. They seem to be more afraid of life than death." —James F. Byrnes

The natural human reaction to fear is to take the path of least resistance and search for security in a full-time job with little flexibility. But is this always the right path? What would life be like if we didn't always succumb to our fear of the unknown?

Jill decided not to go into the necklace business; instead, she became an auditor in a large accounting firm. It's long hours, but it's a secure job. She goes in, they tell her what to do, and she gets it done.

During the "busy" season at the beginning of every year, she works long hours. She knows that she can get a majority of her work done during normal business hours (9 a.m. to 6 p.m.), and she can probably take work home, but she's afraid to leave early because the rest of the team stays late to make a good impression on the partners and clients.

On one particular day, Jill's six-year-old daughter was in a starring role in a play at school. Jill wanted to leave early but struggled to ask her manager because she didn't want to lose her job. "What if the partner finds out? He might tell H.R. to get rid of me!" Jill succumbs to the fear and explains to her daughter over the phone that she won't be able to come to her play because she has to work late.

⁓

Jack, the corporate attorney, finds himself in another meeting where he needs to explain to management the risks of purchasing a business in Fraudonia, which has a bad reputation for a high incidence of kickbacks and fraud.

During the meeting, Jack says, "I would reconsider the purchase. There have been other companies in our industry that have done business in Fraudonia, and a majority of them pulled out because of problems that would have hurt their reputations if they remained there."

The CEO, a bold individual with a history of acting on emotions rather than logic, says, "That's ridiculous! We've run the numbers, and the benefits far outweigh any negative petty bribes that could arise. Besides, we're the leaders in our industry and purchasing that business makes sense."

Taken aback by the brashness of the CEO's statement, and fearing for the security of his own job, Jack nods in agreement along with everyone else.

A majority of people work for others for a living and have to abide by their rules or risk losing their jobs. Those jobs support our families. They pay our mortgages and for our cars. We need to make sure we get along with our colleagues and impress our bosses. This fear of conforming affects all other areas of our lives, whether we like it or not.

A common question we ask everyone when we meet them is: "What do you do for work?" When you think about it, you are really asking them: "What do you do to support the lifestyle you have?" If you lose your job, which is tied to your lifestyle, that loss puts everything else that you have in jeopardy. The questions fly through your mind: How am I going to put food on the table? What about the mortgage? What if my wife thinks I'm a loser and leaves with the kids? You can see how important that job really is.

Another big fear in the workplace is giving presentations. Jerry Seinfeld mused that, at a funeral, most people would rather be in the casket than have to give the eulogy. Getting in front of a crowd is one thing, but giving a presentation to your boss and work colleagues can be one of the most stressful tasks in any job.[15]

Sometimes we don't want to talk to groups for fear of being ridiculed. This happened to you when you were giving a presentation to your sixth-grade class about the history of Native Americans. You were so proud of that presentation and thought you'd nailed it. Then, the teacher poked holes in the facts you presented, which caused the class to laugh at you. You slunk back to your desk dejected, and you vowed never to do a presentation again.

Fast forward thirty years, and as you prepare for

your first presentation in your new role at the XYZ company, you remember when you were ridiculed for what you did in sixth grade. Thoughts run wild and fear enters the scenario:

- What if someone questions me and I don't have the answer?
- What if everyone disagrees with my suggestions?
- What will my boss think about all this disagreement? Will he think I'm a slacker and fire me?

You decide that you should play it safe and not discuss any radical ideas outside the box of what is expected. The fear that arises prevents you from presenting an idea that could save the company thousands—if not millions—of dollars, and it's all based on an event that happened *thirty years ago.*

Another fear in the workplace that arises time and time again is the fear of what shareholders and analysts who report on XYZ company think. The job of the accounting department is to accumulate data coming in for sales made (revenue) and items purchased for production, labor, and consulting services (expenses). In short, if revenues are greater than expenses, you end up with earnings. If expenses are greater than revenue, you end up with losses. This net amount is divided by the number of shares outstanding to arrive at Earnings Per Share, or EPS.

If the company is publicly traded (i.e., it has shares on the NASDAQ, NYSE, or other platforms), analysts dive deep into the company's published financial records to come up with their own predictions of how the company will do in the future. They compare those numbers to the records of the company's competitors as part of their predictions for XYZ company. The result is an EPS prediction for the next quarter, and it is broadcasted through the appropriate news channels. The public sees this, and the stock price could increase based on these predictions and because of the spike in purchases of XYZ company stock.

This puts tremendous pressure on the company to meet or exceed financial expectations. A shortfall of even one cent on anticipated earnings could send the stock in a downward spiral. A date is set for the company's next earnings release, and all shareholders wait with bated breath.

The CFO thinks, "Wow, these analysts are optimistic. How are we going to meet these numbers?" Fear seeps into the CFO's mind, and he thinks: "I have to figure this out or I'll be out of a job. The shareholders and board of directors will certainly point the finger at me for failing to deliver the same results as our competitors. I have to make sure we meet these numbers."

The "creative" accounting begins. Maybe the CFO moves some sales from next quarter into this quarter to increase income, telling himself that it was a done deal anyway. Or maybe he reverses the reserves he set up against some accounts receivable into income with the hope that the customer will pay next year. The numbers are released and everything is good.

How to Deal with Fear in the Workplace
Managing the Demands at Work

Responsibilities at work can be very demanding. You may have a boss who micro-manages but who also runs a team of individuals that needs constant attention. A majority of people at your workplace also have families and forces that pull them in all kinds of directions. How do we deal with conflicts between work and family?

Based on historical data, there is one thing you need to realize: your job is temporary. It may last a year or two. (You might even be out of work next month!) With this in mind, ask yourself a question: What is more important to you? A job that might last a few years, or a family and memories that last a lifetime? I can assure you that I don't think anyone on their death bed will be saying, "I wish I had worked more!"

Based on this reasoning, it would serve you best to face the fear of losing your job and take steps to ensure it doesn't happen. Talk to your immediate boss and ask them if it's okay to leave early to see your daughter's play. There's a good chance they have a daughter or son, too, and would 100 percent understand your request. As long as you are a hard-working employee, you have nothing to fear. Why would they want to lose you? If your boss decides to give you a hard time about leaving for an important family event, talk to their boss. If you still can't get anywhere, start the search for a new job. There are plenty of other companies starving for quality talent, and you will probably get a raise and a better work environment to boot!

Giving Presentations

Standing in front of a crowd is frightening. Even the most experienced speakers encounter fear and beat themselves up afterward on how the presentation should have played out and what they should have said.

According to Craig N. Sawchuk in his article, "Fear of public speaking: How can I overcome it?", here are a couple of quick tips to get over that fear:

- know your topic
- get organized
- practice, and then practice some more
- challenge specific worries
- visualize your success
- do some deep breathing
- focus on your material, not on your audience
- don't fear a moment of silence[16]

If you need to give a presentation to executives in the company, your boss and the direct subordinate to the highest-ranking executive in the meeting should review it first and provide comments. If there is anything out of the ordinary, you will know about it based on their review and can take steps to explain your position in case there is someone who "blows up" at the meeting. Getting management's agreement before you present is key so you will be supported at the meeting.

If you know you have an industry-changing idea, and no one in your company thinks the same, there are three ways you can go:

First: Do nothing and bury the idea. But that is not really giving your best, and it will probably bother you for quite a while. Remember what hockey Hall of Famer Wayne Gretzky said: "You miss 100 percent of the shots you don't take."

Second: Consider expanding on your idea. Ask your

colleagues what information or proof they need to consider it as a good idea for the company. Then, you get their buy-in and increase your chances of getting the idea approved.

Third: Talk to other companies in the industry to see what opportunities may be a good fit for you. As I mentioned above, most jobs are temporary. If you have evidence that supports the validity of your idea and its benefits at another company, get on the phone and start making some calls.

Fourth: Start your own business in the industry. This is risky and challenging, but it could change your life forever. You'll probably get pushback from your spouse, relatives and friends, but this is normal because it will get you out of your comfort zone and make them feel uneasy. (Actually, it will probably force them to look at their own lives and expose fears they have.) Being an entrepreneur is a roller coaster, but guess what? Life is like a heartbeat; it goes up and down. If it's a straight line, you're dead!

Do the Right Thing

There is tremendous pressure to hit your numbers, especially in a publicly-traded company like the company in my previous example. External and internal expectations can put executives in a precarious position, which could force them to "fudge" the numbers for fear of losing their jobs. Also, if executives are heavily invested in the company's stock and are relying on it as a significant part of their nest egg, the fear of having that stock diminish in value adds fuel to the fire of getting the numbers where they need to be, sometimes by any means necessary.

If you're put in an extreme situation that demands a certain result that's unlikely to materialize, speak up. Integrity and clarity in the workplace are key to building a solid company. There have been many people who were fired and even sent to jail for publishing false numbers. What happens to their families while they're gone? What happens down the road when they try to explain what happened to a potential future employer?

Remember: all jobs are temporary. If you feel pressure to communicate something that is not true, and management looks negatively on you, find another place to work. Lack of integrity is not for you!

5

Fear in Relationships

"Of all forms of caution, caution in love is perhaps the most fatal to true happiness."

—**Bertrand Russell**

We all have relationships in our lives. They strengthen and wane as we move along in our journeys. We meet and communicate with new people every day. We pay close attention to these daily encounters so we can size up these new people and determine what they want from us. Sometimes, the fear of getting hurt in a new relationship causes us to be guarded.

Children love making new friends and talking to people. They are naïve and don't think about getting hurt. As I mentioned in the "Fear of Family" chapter, we trust our parents and other family members—especially when we're children—to give us the right advice and guide us in life's journey. When we start school, we begin to form relationships with individuals outside of the family and develop trust in people we are comfortable with.

As we get into our teens, our hormones start to kick in. We have girlfriends and boyfriends who help us take relationships to a deeper level. We bond with our significant other, and we enjoy seeing each other and talking on the phone every day!

Fear in Romantic Relationships

Before Jill met her current husband, she casually dated a couple of guys. One day, she was in a bar with her girlfriends when she noticed a handsome man checking her out from across the bar.

"Whoa, that guy is gorgeous!" she thought. "I'll glance at him every once in a while, and draw him in."

He finally came over and introduced himself. "I'm sorry, but have we met before? I'm Rick."

"Hello, Rick," Jill said. "I'm not sure if we've met before."

The conversation continued, and he asked for her number. They went on a date, and Jill had a fantastic time. One date led to two; then they began seeing other every week and talking every day. Eventually, Rick and Jill moved in together.

"Wow. This guy is the one!" Jill thought.

They went on vacations together, exercised together, and spent lazy Sundays together.

The relationship progressed, and after a year, Jill believed they'd proved their relationship was solid. She began to wonder how to discuss with Rick what might be next for them. She envisioned the two of them in their beautiful house in their upscale neighborhood with their two kids (girl and boy, of course).

One day, she noticed Rick's phone buzzing. She looked at the message and saw it was from someone named Sarah.

I HAD A GREAT TIME LAST NIGHT AND I CAN'T WAIT TO BE WITH YOU AGAIN.

It was as if a heavy weight crashed onto Sarah's chest. Who the hell was Sarah? She picked up Rick's phone, went into the other room, and handed it to him.

"Who is Sarah?" she shouted.

Rick's face turned white. "Uh ... uh ... she's a work colleague," he stuttered.

"Get out!" Jill screamed.

Rick grabbed his keys and bolted for the door. Jill felt as if a knife had plunged into her. She curled up on the floor, sobbing. Eventually, she told her friends what happened, and they consoled her as she cried. Rick came for his stuff the next day, and then he was gone.

It took a while for Jill to get over Rick and to get back into the dating scene. Once she returned, she was guarded with every man she met. She was so guarded, in fact, that she only ever went on one date with each one. Even if she liked the guy, she feared getting hurt again.

The fear of infidelity is very real. Marketing from companies that show bikini models as wives and ripped athletes as husbands doesn't help. Two people get together as a result of the "new" feeling that excites both. But as time goes on, that feeling slowly evaporates for many people, and we look to others for the next relationship. Jill opened up and trusted Rick. She was already married to him in her mind! Then, her world came crashing down.

Jill thought, "What if I *do* find 'Mr. Right' one day, and what if he leaves me like Rick did? How can I trust that anyone is ever going to stick around after what happened to me? I'll probably end up alone in an apartment somewhere for the rest of my life."

This line of thinking leads to the fear of abandonment, which therapists say is the number one fear people have in relationships. When we enter into relationships, it's because we want to share our lives with someone. But we fear relationships, too, because we fear being abandoned by someone we care about. In her article "3 Relationship Fears Literally Every Person Has, Because You're Not Alone," Annie Foskett explains: "So it makes perfect sense that the fear of being abandoned and losing our partner is the most painful for us."[17]

Another fear that arises in relationships is when we think that we're not good enough for our partner. Jill was shocked when Rick was drawn to someone else. She wondered whether something might be wrong with her. Why would he want Sarah instead of her?

A third fear that arises is that we will not get our own needs met by our partners. We fear they won't be able to take care of us as we believe they should. We fear not being heard or understood, or not having our basic emotional needs met.[18]

Fear-Based Parenting

Where are my kids?

Make sure you text me once every hour while you're out tonight with your friends.

Make sure you get straight As this semester because you need to get into XYZ college.

One term that refers to parents who operate in this manner is "helicopter" parenting. These are parents who are overprotective and—more generally—over-involved in their children's lives. In his article, "The Many Shades of Fear-Based Parenting," Peter Gray writes: "They're [helicopter parents] convinced that danger lurks around every corner, and so they guard and advise their child at every turn."[19]

"These parents have difficulty letting go, even when their children are adults, perhaps partly because their offspring actually seem to need extra help, as they developed habits of helplessness resulting from all the previous helicoptering. These parents continue to want to know all the details of their adult children's lives and to offer unsolicited advice as the latter pursue higher education or careers or start to raise a family of their own."[20]

There are also "snowplow" parents. "These are parents who use their wealth, status, and inflated sense of privilege to clear the path for their children. Much of their effort is aimed at getting their children into and through the most elite college possible, or the most prestigious and well-paying *career* because these are parents who place great value on the outward appearance of success."[21]

In addition to "plowing" the way, an incidental outcome is to inflate their children's egos.

One infamous example of "snowplow" parenting involved Hollywood actresses who were found to have paid millions of dollars in bribes to get their kids into some of the nation's top universities. These parents were obsessed with maintaining their movie-star status and were determined to get their kids into prestigious schools, no matter the cost. For them, fear arose through wondering what everyone would think if their own kids failed to accomplish what other kids did.[22]

Parenting is not an easy task. Being a "helicopter" and/or "snowplow" parent might come from a place of caring, but it only leads to problems as our kids get older.

Fear of Letting Down Friends

When Jack graduated from law school, he started with a big law firm and quickly rose through the ranks because management saw his potential. One day, he met an old childhood friend, Sam, after work. They'd been best friends through high school and kept in touch after, even though they'd gone to different colleges.

That day after work, Sam asked Jack to invest in his "revolutionary idea" that was going to "turn the social media world upside down." Jack had saved some money during his brief career and he trusted Sam. So, a few days later, Jack wired Sam a large sum of cash as an investment in the new venture. Sam emailed Jack and told him that he was excited and that he would get the appropriate documents to him shortly.

A week went by, then two weeks, then a month. Jack heard nothing from Sam. Finally, he called Sam, but Sam's number had been disconnected. Puzzled, Jack emailed Sam, but the email bounced with the message: address not found. "What the heck is happening?" Jack thought. "Where is this guy?" Finally, after work one evening, he drove to Sam's apartment and knocked on the door. No answer. He saw an envelope sticking out from under the door that read: Final Eviction Notice.

Jack was hit with a heavy weight. Sam was gone, and with him, Jack's money.

"How could he do this to me? What kind of 'friend' does something like this?" Jack exclaimed.

He never heard from or saw Sam again, and Jack resolved never to lend money to anyone again.

Many of us have experienced something like this. We trust someone so much that we don't even question them when they ask us for a loan or investment. When we get burned, the fear of loss of our hard-earned money stops us from trusting anyone again.

How to Deal with Fear in Relationships
Trust Your Partner

The most common problem with any type of negative event that has arisen in the past is that it will create a negative expectation for present or future opportunities. A lot of people fall into this trap and let great opportunities (or people) slip away because of the fear that the same negative result will happen again.

If you start questioning your partner about their fidelity without a shred of evidence, stop! You need to pause and consider why these feelings have arisen. Are you bringing up some old relationship that went sour because of your partner's cheating? Or is it caused by another incident in your life in which someone you trusted let you down?

It's a mistake to let your past dictate how you react to a present situation. I had a partner in the past who constantly accused me of staring at other women and cheating on her when that was absolutely not the case. The relationship ended, and she lost an awesome guy because of her inability to trust me. Constant accusations of cheating when there's no basis for doing so will cause serious damage. Eventually, your significant other will get fed up and leave. Trust is a critical element in the creation of a lasting relationship.

You should listen to your gut when you can't seem to pinpoint where this fear of infidelity is coming from. Talk to your partner and let them know how you're feeling. It could be an opportunity for them to get out of the relationship (which is a good thing for both of you). It could also be something that may cause some uncomfortable conversations in the beginning but may bring you closer together in the end. The key to any healthy relationship is open and honest communication, and respect for each other. If your gut is eventually right about your partner, karma will eventually be served to them.

Let Your Kids Live

It is natural for parents to look out for their kids and keep them away from the "dangers" that they confront every day. However, we do not do our children any favors by letting our exaggerated fears of dangers constrict their lives in ways that remove their joy and disempower them so they don't develop the coping skills needed to deal with actual dangers.[23]

Of course, we should steer our kids in the right direction if we see perils that need to be avoided, but we also need to trust that they will find the right way and avoid most dangers on their own. This is an essential part of growing up. A child tries something, fails, then learns what not to do in the future. It's the only way they will learn, and it builds character to handle difficult scenarios that crop up in the future. It is "life education" on their way to becoming adults. They will be stronger, live more meaningful lives, and be great role models for their kids.

Know Your Friends

Fear may arise when it comes to very personal things, like when Sam felt obligated to lend money to his friend Jack.

Shakespeare wrote, "For loan oft loses both itself and friend."[24] If you lend money to a friend or family member, beware that you may not get your money back, and your relationship may never go back to normal. This will cause tension between you and the borrower, and it may also cause guilt, remorse, and anger. That being said, you have to know to whom you are lending the money, if they are trustworthy and have the means to pay it back, and what the loan is for. Taking the negative results from a loan made in the past and applying it to a current situation is not necessarily the answer.

Trusting a friend is natural, and if that trust is broken, the friendship will break as well. There is a school of thought that you should never lend money to a friend or relative, and I would agree with this in general. Have a frank conversation to determine what their actual needs are to see if you can help in some way other than lending money. If there are no other sources for the funds, point out the consequences to the friendship if your friend doesn't pay back your money. This may "flip a switch" in the other person's head, and they may back off as they didn't realize the potential consequences or problems that would arise because of the loan.

Midpoint Fear Checkup

Congratulations! You've made it halfway through Crushing Your Fear.

Here are a couple of questions to think about:

1. Are you fearless and living your life according to your dreams? Is there someone or something holding you back? If there is, what will you do to free yourself in order to move forward?

2. Have extended or immediate family members shot your ideas down? How did that make you feel? What are you going to do to resurrect those ideas and test them?

3. Do you have a good idea that you want to execute, but you haven't done anything to develop it yet? Do you find yourself over-analyzing and procrastinating to the point that you put that idea on a shelf?

4. Are you afraid to ask that girl or guy out for fear of rejection? What is your plan to push through and finally act?

5. Has a failure or setback in the past kept you from doing that thing you really want to do for fear of failing again? What steps are you taking to put the past in the past and move forward?

6. Are you letting your work invade time with your family to the point that you miss key life events? What steps are you taking to make sure that doesn't happen anymore?

7. When you speak to an audience, are you confident in your material and delivery? If not, are

you getting the coaching you need to do a "killer" presentation?

8. Are you ethical and honest in all areas of your life? How would you feel if someone was not honest with you?

9. Do you have a partner and friends whom you can trust? Do you have a hard time trusting them? Why?

10. Are you guiding your kids loosely, or are you smothering them with unbreakable rules?

6

Fear of Social Media

"We all enjoy dipping our toe in the cold water of fear." —**Alfred Hitchcock**

Social media is pervasive in our lives. Most of us are constantly looking at Facebook and Instagram to see what's happening in everyone's lives. We also go out of our way to snap perfect pictures of ourselves so we can post online and get "likes." These "likes" are a sort of instant gratification and affirmation for us, aren't they? But it's unsettling when we don't get a lot of "likes," and fear arises. We wonder if something's wrong with our account settings—or worse—whether we're not quite as good-looking as we thought.

We have thoughts and plan to put pictures, stories—even videos—onto our social media sites. We set ourselves up for all the glory and attention. But when those things don't materialize, we begin to question whether we're good enough. We fear expressing what we really feel going forward and envy others who get thousands of likes.

When Jill was in college, she noticed that there were a lot of influencers popping up on social media. She thought, "These women are getting thousands of likes when they post their pictures. Sure, they look trashy, but they're getting a lot of attention! I look good. I can do that too!"

Jill was quite attractive. She started posting photos in revealing outfits, and she got two thousand likes overnight. Then, she got several messages from companies asking her to model their products, and they offered to pay her for her time.

"Absolutely!" she responded.

A couple of months passed, and she reached 20,000 likes per post. Her self-confidence went through the roof, and she decided to start posting videos of herself playing guitar and singing because it was her true passion. She aimed to get 40,000 likes with her first video.

She recorded the video and posted it that evening. But when she woke the next day, she only had fifty likes. She was dumbfounded. What if her clients saw that? They could cancel her contracts, which would mean no more money. How would she pay her rent if that happened? She knew she needed to take down the video, but she'd also grown weary of posting provocative photos of herself. She didn't know the best way forward.

In his article, "Dopamine, Smartphones & You: A battle for your time," Trevor Haynes writes:

"Smartphones and the social media platforms they support are turning us into *bona fide* addicts." As a matter of fact, platforms like Facebook, Twitter, Snapchat, and Instagram utilize the same neural circuitry leveraged by slot machines and cocaine to keep us "hooked" on using their products for long periods of time."[25]

In the same article, Haynes writes: "Dopamine is a chemical produced by our brains that plays a major role in motivating behavior. It's released when we take a bite of delicious food, when we have sex, after we exercise, and—importantly—when we have successful social interactions."[26]

The human brain contains dopamine "pathways," or connections between different parts of the brain, that act as highways for chemical messages called neurotransmitters. There are "reward pathways" that have been shown to be associated with most cases of addiction. They are responsible for the release of dopamine in various parts of the brain, which shapes the activity of those areas. In particular, they reinforce the association between a particular stimulus or sequence of behaviors and the feel-good reward that follows.

While not as intense as a hit of cocaine, social media "likes" and positive emojis will similarly result in a release of dopamine, encouraging similar behavior. Smartphones are a convenient way to perpetuate this behavior.

How do you feel when you realize that you misplaced your phone? If you said it makes you afraid or panicked, you're not alone. Adults in the U.S. spend an average of two to four hours per day tapping, typing, and swiping on their devices. That adds up to more than 2,600 daily touches. Most of us have become so intimately connected to our digital lives that we sometimes feel our phones vibrating in our pockets when they aren't even there. It's kind of like Pavlov's discovery that dogs will salivate even when their bowls are empty. Based on this, we can conclude that our smartphones have become part of us.[27]

In the article, "What Is Social Media Addiction?", Jena Hilliard writes: "Research has shown that there is an undeniable link between social media use, negative mental health, and low self-esteem."[28]

While social media has some benefits, using it too frequently can make people feel increasingly unhappy and isolated. People fear what others will think of them if they post pictures of their "mediocre" existence as compared to the flawless, filtered, and edited online versions of others. This contributes significantly to a negative perception of self. This pattern also increases the risk of developing mental health issues such as anxiety and depression. Constantly comparing oneself to others can lead to feelings of self-consciousness, or a need for perfectionism and order, which often leads to social anxiety disorder.

> "Another aspect of social anxiety triggered by online media use is the fear of missing out (FOMO), the extreme fear of not being included or missing a social event. Users may see pictures of parties to which they were not invited, or glimpses of fun outings that they were unable to attend because of work or school obligations, and experience anxiety that no one misses them as a result

— or fear that they will be forgotten since they're not there. FOMO can take a toll on self-esteem and lead to compulsive checking of social media platforms to ensure that an individual isn't missing out on anything, which can cause problems in the workplace and in the classroom."[29]

Another real fear, especially in children and teens, is online bullying. This "cyberbullying" by adolescents has occurred in the past, but social media has amplified bullying to its highest levels. Teenagers are at particular risk for cyberbullying through social media. In addition to face-to-face bullying, the spreading and posting of non-consensual explicit pictures is a form of cyberbullying that has gained popularity in recent years. Twenty-five percent of teens say they have been sent explicit images they didn't request, while seven percent say explicit photos of themselves have been shared without their consent. These factors have contributed to increased levels of anxiety in teens and adolescents.[30]

Social media can also cause anxiety in adults as well.

In addition to his other duties at his company, Jack was tasked to develop a presence on social media because he knew what content would work for his company and what would keep them out of trouble. The issue, however, was that he didn't have a lot of experience with social media.

"I'm not a marketing or advertising guy," Jack claimed. "This whole social media thing is a fad and for kids anyway. Why should I waste my time with it? I think it's a waste of money as well. And they want me to make videos walking around the office interviewing employees and saying great things about the company. I don't know what I'm doing!"

Jack's fear of the unknown social media world led him to procrastinate coming up with a plan to create an online platform for his company. His line of thinking and his fear of social media could be a huge detriment to the company. Ignoring the power and ramp-up of social media's relevance is not a good strategy.

How to Deal with Fear in Social Media

Limit Your Time on It

Tony Watley, an entrepreneur and coach, was on my Crushing Your Fear podcast to speak about social media's attention-grabbing impact on society. Based on his marketing background, he said this: "If the social media outlets can run an ad with a shocking headline that gets you to click through, they will make millions by propagating this fear."

It's easy to get lost in random videos or ads that pop up on your accounts. But like Tony Watley said, those ads are put there for a purpose. You're meant to be captivated. Look at headlines for what they are and consider the source before you get caught in that trap. Don't give in to the temptation to click on intriguing pictures or headlines. They're called clickbait for a reason!

But with all the time-wasting temptations available via social media, how do you actually limit your time on it?

Write down how much daily time you spend on social media in addition to the time spent texting. When you look at it, you'll be surprised at all the time you spent on these activities.

Smartphones also give weekly data reports on how much time you've spent on them and whether that time is an increase or decrease from the week prior. What would your day look like if you set aside time on your calendar to catch up on social media, direct messages (DMs), and texts rather than spending minute after minute across an entire day doing those things? It will be hard at first, but you'll be much more productive and pay more attention to the things that matter.

Have a Plan: Be Yourself

People know when someone is not being real with them. They see through the theatrics and flashy stuff in online posts. You may be able to get a large following by playing into popular trends (i.e., photos of yourself in low-cut dresses or pictures with exotic cars), but if that isn't your authentic self, you'll run into trouble. In our example, Jill had a major problem because she created a "character" that wasn't her true self, and she got stuck doing something she didn't like.

If you make a video, speak from the heart. Take pictures of yourself in everyday life, not in some parking lot at a country club in front of a Ferrari. Show your followers you're human and you make mistakes. Tell them your story. Tell them about real-life experiences, the good and bad. People will relate to you more, and you'll develop the following you want. From there, just offer to help them any way you can. Give constantly, and you will receive great things back!

Limit Your Kids' Time on Social Media

Kids' brains and social skills continue to develop through their teens. Unfortunately, most of them are addicted to their phones and tablets because they spend many hours each day texting, posting, and communicating with other individuals. These communications could be harmless interactions with friends, or they could be something more negative. Pictures of "perfect" families and people may trigger low self-esteem and depression. They also may be exposed to images and content that is downright disturbing. All of this leads to a significant decrease of in-person social-interaction skills.

Parents need to get involved with what their kids are looking at and the sites they have access to. Parental controls are available on home Wi-Fi networks, through apps, and on the actual devices. Barring that, if you sense that something is troubling your kids, talk to them. Trust and an open line of communication are key to successful parent/child relationships. Also, take the phones away for part of the day and tell them to go outside to play with their friends!

Get Your Company a LinkedIn Page

Companies that have been successful with traditional media outlets (i.e., TV, radio, and magazines) might find that developing a social media presence is challenging. But they may also see that their competitors are thriving on social media and taking market share away. Social media isn't a fad. It's increasing its reach and impact daily. In fact, several major department store chains have been put out of business due to their failure to pivot to an online presence.

Social media is also the perfect arena for a disgruntled customer to trash a company's reputation. Therefore, it's critical to monitor social media to address any negative comments or accusations before they damage a company's reputation.

There are a few critical steps a company should take to jump into the social media universe:

1. Create and implement a social media policy.

    a. Educate your employees on what social media is and why it's important.

    b. You should give them guidelines on what is and what isn't appropriate to post on social media as a representative of the company.

    c. There should also be a procedure in place to deal with negative situations like a mob of people trashing your company online because of a post taking sides on a controversial subject.

2. Develop a social media strategy to promote your brand and product, and communicate its value for people. You should create solid content that reaches your target audience, set goals that you wish to achieve, and create a budget to get you there. When you start seeing the results of this strategy, your fears will melt away. (And you get your company into the new millennium. Congratulations!)[31]

7

Fear in the Media

"The more the media peddled fear, the more the people lost the ability to believe in one another."   —**Bernard Beckett**

Fear in the media is very real. It is used to generate an emotion that can motivate you to do or not do something. In America, particularly throughout the last several years, the media has used fear to divide us.

We question whether the information we receive from media sources is accurate or fake. There are several different media outlets that are unquestionably biased in their views—both liberal and conservative. It seems that the more national and widespread the media outlet is, the more biased it becomes. But what does this fear instilled by the media actually do to us mentally and physically?

Fear-based news stories prey on our anxieties. Constant exposure to negative news can actually lead to depression and impact our mental and physical state.

In the *Psychology Today* article, "If It Bleeds, It Leads: Understanding Fear-Based Media," Deborah Serani writes: "In previous decades, the journalistic mission was to report the news as it actually happened, with fairness, balance, and integrity. However, capitalistic motives associated with journalism have forced much of today's TV news to look to the spectacular, the stirring, and the controversial as news stories. It's no longer a race to break the story first or get the facts right. Instead, it's to acquire good ratings in order to get advertisers, so that profits soar."[32]

Today's news is primarily panic-driven and delivered twenty-four hours a day. News outlets use programming to achieve two objectives: 1) grab the viewer's attention via a teaser; and 2) persuade the viewer that the solution for reducing the identified fear will be in the news story. If a teaser asks, "How can you protect yourself and your family from the latest virus?", a viewer will likely tune in to get the up-to-date information on which facemasks work better than others and where you should wear them.[33]

The Media and Fear of a Virus

Jill's college friend, Karen, eventually got married and had two kids. Recently, Karen noticed some stories about an outbreak of a new, rapidly spreading virus, according to the Global News Network (GNN), which is her news source of choice. Then, she started seeing headlines scrolling across the bottom of the screen that proclaimed thousands of new cases of the virus were appearing in cities across the U.S.

"Oh my gosh," she thought. "What's going on?"

Her phone began to buzz with notifications from her favorite social media site, PlaceHook, alerting her to stories about the virus published by GNN and other national and global news outlets. These same sources advised her to keep up with their notifications so she could stay updated as they received new information.

As time went by, and news about the virus became scarier, she began to see never-ending ads about face masks and where to get them. "Buy now" links were embedded in the online ads that ran alongside terrifying stories about exposure to the virus and the uptick in deaths caused by it.

Breaking news stories are usually communicated using words that stir up fear in us. This fear overload causes a sort of paralysis, a "freezing" instead of fight or flight. We become glued to the TV or our phones, our gazes riveted to the words that scroll across the screen. Now, the journalists have our attention.

The need to get-the-story-to-get-the-ratings often causes reporters to bypass fact-checking. As news released by a reporter develops and attracts more attention, the reporter subsequently corrects the inaccuracies and missing elements that were missing from the original story. As the process of fact-finding continually changes, so does the news story. What journalists first reported with intense emotion or sensationalism is no longer accurate, which leaves the viewer with a fragmented sense of what's real. This psychological effect can trigger feelings of hopelessness and helplessness, two emotions that can worsen depression. The COVID-19 news cycle and projections of "millions of lives being lost" caused Karen to panic. But as time went on, those numbers were revised downwards significantly.

The Media and Fear of Terrorism

The media coverage of terrorism has also been a source of fear in recent history. In an average year, terrorism accounts for approximately four percent of the total homicide deaths in the world. But it is given a lot of news coverage. A majority of those deaths happen in war zones (mainly the Middle East). However, the events of 9/11 will remain with us for a long time. Any time we hear about terrorism, we automatically recall that it can happen here in the U.S. as well, and that realization keeps us guarded.

The media's coverage of terrorist events is, unfortunately in line with the terrorists' objectives. They want to maximize the coverage they get in certain populations so as to intimidate as many people as possible and recruit the largest number of supporters.[34]

An additional practice used by the media that heightens fear is the use of the crawl, which is the scrolling breaking-news headline ticker that appears at the bottom of your screen. The crawl first began to appear after the 9/11 attack on the World Trade Center in New York. Everyone was glued to their TV screens, desperate for as much information as they could get because the fear of another attack was very real.

Though the initial terror following 9/11 faded, the crawl never went away. The multitasking required to read the crawls and comprehend the actual newscast comes easy to some viewers, whereas other viewers report feeling over-stimulated. The crawls frequently contain fear-driven material that broadsides unsuspecting viewers. But there is an addictive quality to them as well that prompts us to continue to watch. Focused eyeballs lead to longer attention spans, which leads to increased revenue.[35]

Crimes are constantly communicated through the media to stoke fear. In the article, "Mass Media, Crime, and the Discourse of Fear," author David L. Altheide writes: "Objective indicators of risk and danger in American life suggest that most U.S. citizens are healthier, safer, and live more predictable lives than at any time in history, yet numerous surveys indicate these same citizens perceive that their lives are very dangerous." This perception is enforced through a media stream of crime reporting across the world, which leads us to believe that danger and risk are a central feature to everyday life.[36]

How to Deal with Fear in Media

Negative news is prevalent in media because it attracts attention, and attention helps sell ads. But constantly hearing and watching negative news is destructive to our own well-being. So, with that in mind, here are some tips on how to overcome the power of fear-based media.

Look at the Situation Objectively

One of the most effective ways to get a handle on our negativity bias is to look at the situation objectively. Even in the worst of circumstances, we can find silver linings. Develop some mental toughness and you will survive your circumstances rather than have your circumstances change you.

Read Beyond the Headline

Fear-based news stories prey on our anxieties and then hold us hostage. Cable news stations and newspapers work with headline consultants and train their editors to pull together headlines that will induce fear.

Whether it's a newscast or newspaper, take the time to read beyond the headline. If you read the article to the end, you'll discover that the headlines are often misleading or sensationalist. The headline highlights the most negative point of the story, and if we read the *entire* story, we can usually conclude that the headline is more of an exaggeration than fact.

Listen to Your Gut

In 2020, when the COVID-19 quarantine had just begun, we saw how fear led to a toilet paper shortage. Was it logical for people to buy a year's supply of toilet paper? Of course not! We do irrational things when we don't understand events that could threaten our safety and health. The herd mentality (also known as mob mentality) means that people think and imitate the same behaviors as those around them and often ignore common sense in the process.

Bottom line? Check your gut. Is this something you're doing because you need some element of control in your out-of-control life? Is this something you're doing because others are doing it? Whom should we trust when given a choice based on so many unknown variables, fearmongers or fact-based scientists who have spent a lifetime studying the effects of pandemics? Take a break and figure it out.

Know Your Triggers

We all have the fight-or-flight response when confronted with something that is not in our normal routine. When we hear about a virus killing thousands of people, we naturally grab a mask and head indoors. We turn on the TV to get more information. We keep watching because we want *more* information. But that negative information is the fuel that feeds the fear.

Multiple guests on my Crushing Your Fear podcast have said that one way to deal with fear is to move toward the threat. In the *Advisorpedia* article, "How To Overcome The Power Of Fear-Based Media," LaRae Quy writes: "The more we learn about it [fear], the less power it has over us." If you see a news story that tells us X about the threat of a virus and what it has actually done, take the time to consider the source of the story, and do your own research to verify the information. Once you have this information, make your own decision on how to deal with it.[37]

Turn the TV Off and Put the Phone Away

The media needs to return to a sense of proportion, conscience, and—most important—truth-telling. Until that happens, help inoculate yourself against feeling overwhelmed by making a plan such as the one described in "If It Bleeds: It Leads: Understanding Fear-Based Media":

- Consider limiting your exposure to media. Give yourself a set time once or twice a day to check in on local and global happenings.

- Consider choosing print media for your information-gathering rather than visual media. This can reduce the likelihood that you get exposed to emotionally laden material.

- Remember that you have the power to turn off the TV, leave a website, or change the radio station. Don't let yourself be passive when you feel media is overwhelming you.

- Know that other people will have a different tolerance for media stories and their details. If someone is discussing a story too much for your own comfort level, walk away or communicate your distress.

- Consider having an electronic-free day, and take in the simpler things in life.[38]

Miguel Garcia, serial entrepreneur and founder of Natural Choice, was a guest on episode thirteen of my Crushing Your Fear podcast, and he said this: "Fear lives in the past or in the future. We choose to bring that fear into our present."

The media bombards us with fear-based headlines on a daily basis, but it's our choice whether those fear-inducing stories become part of our present. We need to be aware of the media's tactics and make our own decisions on how those stories will affect us.

8

Fear in Education

"Fears are educated into us, and can, if we wish, be educated out."   —**Karl Augustus Menninger**

The fear of education starts in preschool and kindergarten. We go from the safety of running around free at home, to the anxiety of traveling by bus every day to the local school to spend the whole day with strangers. Then, we are instructed by an adult teacher on what we should do and when we should do it. We even have to hand our drawings in to the teacher who returns them to us with a smiley face or a sad face. When we get sad faces, the teacher explains that we need to color "within the lines" because big boys and girls do that. We think to ourselves that we have to do better because we don't want to upset or disappoint our parents.

The fear begins.

We complete kindergarten and move into higher grades where we have to take tests and get graded on a scale of A (Excellent) through F (Failure). All the "smart" kids get As and are praised by the teacher, while all the kids who get Fs are made fun of.

"Mom and Dad say they want to see straight As on my report card," we think. "I'd better figure this out, because I'm not a loser like the kids who get Fs."

Jill's son Johnny had to be "observed" so he could be admitted into a prestigious preschool program. The school boasted that 90 percent of kids enrolled in their program eventually made it into Ivy League schools. Amazing!

"Now, Johnny, make sure you do the very best you can and listen very closely to what Mr. Jones asks you and give him the right answer, okay?" says Johnny's mom. "Don't fool around because we need you to get into this school so you can be successful."

"If Johnny screws up and doesn't get in, our family will look like losers," Jill thinks to herself.

By the way, Johnny just turned four years old last month.

We can see how fear plays a big role in education. Kids are afraid of what their parents and classmates will think if they don't get straight As. Parents fear what neighbors will think of them if their kids don't get accepted into the "prestigious" school.

On a personal note, we brought one of my daughters to one of the "prestigious" preschools to see how they assessed her. Unfortunately, they concluded that she would not be a good fit for their program. She is in seventh grade at the time of this writing, and she has an overall grade point average of 98 percent and is consistently on the principal's list.

The fear that is instilled by the education system into parents and in the attendees of that system is real. According to the article, "Helping students overcome their fear of failure," which appeared on the *European Association for International Education* website, research has shown that students don't fear failure itself; they fear the "negative consequences associated with under-achieving."[39]

The same article states that there are three general groups of observable consequences:

- **Personal:** Students feel ashamed about their inability and incompetence. They experience hurt from having to acknowledge their shortcomings and limitations. In addition, they have feelings of guilt and worthlessness.

- **Interpersonal:** Students don't want to disappoint their parents. They also fear receiving ridicule from classmates and losing their teacher's trust and support.

- **"Career-related:** Having decreased chances on the job market and decreased chances to have a decent income and appropriate social status."[40]

There are good aspects of having a structured education, and one can say that fear plays a positive role in these situations. For example, I went to an all-boys Catholic high school where "nonsense" was not tolerated. By nonsense, I mean talking while your professor was giving a lecture or being late for class. If you slipped up, you got detention. That meant you had to stay after school—and be absolutely silent—for two hours in a classroom with other offenders. In extreme cases, you would get a week's worth of detentions and possibly have to come in on weekends! Although not an optimal way of handling things, it forced you to think twice before you acted out again.

Another good aspect of a structured education is that it provides a safe learning environment with the support of students' teachers and classmates. When the COVID-19 pandemic hit, my daughters were forced to stay home and have classes virtually through online group calls. My youngest, who was eight years old, had difficulties with this. She would run out of her room crying that she didn't know what to do next in certain online lessons, and her teacher was not physically there to guide and reassure her. My other daughters and I stepped in to help her and she got back on track. When I asked her a few weeks later if she was caught up on her homework, she said, "Yes, Dad!" So, I let it go.

Unfortunately, the teacher reported a month later that my daughter failed to submit any homework during that month! We intervened and got her caught up, but in the end, I observed that my daughter feared how to act or even learn without having a teacher in the room with her.

How to Deal with Fear in Education

Calm the Fear in Your Kids

School can be a scary place for kids because they can feel vulnerable in a competitive environment outside the safety of their home. When you introduce the A through F grading system, fuel is added to the fears of inadequacy and disappointing others.

Consistently check with your kids to see how they are doing in school, and communicate with their teachers on a regular basis. Talk to your kids to see what they are worried about, then help them identify and overcome those fears:

- Are your kids worried about disappointing their parents, classmates, or teachers? Ask them why they are worried. Did someone say something that created an expectation that, if not met, might cause disappointment? Keep digging to find out the root cause. Maybe it was something that you said that was taken out of context and blown up to large proportions. Let them talk through their feelings and analyze with them to dispel any myths they may have created. Also, reinforce that you support them as long as they give it 100 percent. Encourage them not to worry about what others think.

- Are your kids worried about career opportunities if they don't get into a certain school or get interviewed or hired upon graduation into that prestigious company because of their grades? Talk with your kids and explain that a high GPA does not automatically guarantee success. It may open a few doors, but if the person who gets accepted on grades is not well-rounded with both intelligence and interpersonal skills, they won't get very far in whatever company they end up in. Encourage them to take a look at what they are passionate about and explore starting a "side hustle," or maybe they ought to just jump in full-time to see if they could make a living at it. You may be saving them years of mediocrity and anguish over the "safe" path they chose instead of following their dreams.

♦ Do your kids have an "A-grade-or-I-failed" mentality? This could create a tremendous expectation and put pressure on them to achieve that A. It could lead to extreme behavior that could set them up for great disappointment if they don't achieve that goal. Explain to them that while it's optimal to aim for and achieve that A grade, life doesn't end if we miss that mark. In fact, many successful people have failed time and time again, but what made them successful is that they bounced back and kept at it until they succeeded. This message is one of the greatest gifts you can give to your child.

YOU Need to Calm Down

Take a look at how you speak to your children, and be mindful not to unintentionally set them up for failure. Creating consequences or expressing your disappointment if they don't get As in every class imparts a huge amount of stress on them. While big goals and dreams are no doubt the way to live life, these are children, and they take everything literally. You could be setting them up for big issues down the road. Some better advice might be: "I want you to give 100 percent all the time in every class, and no matter what happens, if you can tell me that you gave 100 percent, I will support you!"

Another thing I see parents do is live the life that they wished they had through their kids. If you wanted to be an engineer, but you never had the opportunity to do so, don't force your kid to attend the best engineering school if they aren't interested in math or science! This will definitely set them up for a life of regret and turmoil. How will you feel about yourself then? Ask them what their passion is and steer them toward that.

My daughter is fantastic at drawing and wanted to get into a specialized high school geared toward the Arts. We supported her 100 percent, and she got in. My other daughter loves acting and being on stage. We will not tell her that she should wake up because the chances of becoming famous are slim to none. How could we possibly know what her capabilities are? We are getting her the training and exposure she needs to follow her dream, and that's what we *should* do as parents.

9

Fear of Government

> "Our government has kept us in a perpetual state of fear—kept us in a continuous stampede of patriotic fervor—with the cry of grave national emergency." —**Douglas MacArthur**

Tribalism, or the behavior and attitudes that stem from strong loyalty to one's own tribe or social group, has been an inherent part of human history. As humans, we have an evolutionary advantage that has prevented us from repeating the dangerous experiences of other humans. In the *MarketWatch* article, "Opinion: A neuroscientist explains how politicians and the media use fear to make us hate without thinking," author Arash Javanbakht writes: "We have a tendency to trust our tribe mates and authorities, especially when it comes to danger. For example, parents and wise old men told us not to eat a special plant or we would die, or not to go to an area in the woods or we would be hurt."[41]

"Tribalism is the biological loophole that many politicians have banked on for a long time: tapping into our fears and tribal instincts." [42] They claim that their political party will protect us, and they instill the fear that the other party will hurt us. This is an abuse of power that can wreak havoc on the people the government is meant to represent, and it creates groups of people that do not communicate. Rather, they learn to hate one another without even knowing each other.

Over the course of history, governments and religion become one, and individuals were required to conform or fear being imprisoned or worse. The pharaohs in ancient Egypt, for example, claimed to be gods, and their subjects feared the wrath of their alleged supernatural powers. This generated a "priestly" element of fear whereby individuals were instructed to practice good behavior in order to receive salvation in the afterlife. The combination of "warrior" and "priestly" aspects of government became a successful recipe to sustain governments for thousands of years.

Governments then evolved into protectors of their people, and as societies modernized, that protection expanded to areas such as unemployment and food safety. Citizens began to believe that they *needed* the government to keep them safe, and they feared what might happen if the government failed to do that.

Here are several examples of the use of fear by governments and their consequences throughout history, as reported in the *CBC News* article, "Fear in politics: 5 examples through history:

- **Peloponnesian War**: Long ago, when Athens had bad relations with Sparta, a fear tactic used by Athens backfired on them. Instead of Athens telling its people that they needed to fear Sparta, they advised Sparta that they needed to be afraid of them. This caused a backlash that resulted in a war-ending with Sparta's defeat of Athens.

- **Nazism**: Biased news broadcast by the Nazi government in Germany caused the population to believe that attack on them by outside forces would be imminent. The battle cry and subsequent war resulted in catastrophic loss of life and left their nation in shambles.

- **Stalin and Mao**: These two communist leaders ruled through fear and propaganda. The government's rules were largely unquestioned, which led to many costly mistakes, such as the Great Leap Forward in China, which resulted in tens of millions of deaths and led to the Great Chinese Famine, the largest famine in human history.

  In the Soviet Union in the mid-twentieth century, Lysenkoism, which was a political campaign led by Trofim Lysenko against science-based agriculture, led to the dismissal or imprisonment of more than three thousand mainstream biologists and the execution of numerous scientists to suppress scientific opponents. Both programs were disastrous for those countries.[43]

During the COVID-19 pandemic (just past its peak at the time of this writing), governments' roles were the focus of every citizen in every nation. We were glued to our TVs (as I briefly discussed in the

Fear of Media and Fear of Social Media chapters). We asked ourselves, "Am I allowed to leave my house?", "Can I open my store again?", "Will I be able to see my gravely ill parent one more time before they pass?"

If we did venture out, we saw flashing signs warning us to "Wear a Mask in Public," "Wash Your Hands," and "Flatten the Curve." Fearful times, indeed.

> "Hey, it's an election year and I better register to vote," Jack thinks. "But whom should I vote for? One political party says they're on my side, but my brother was forced to shut his store during the pandemic and isn't sure how his business will survive.
>
> "The same party that's running my area says it's a "federal government decision" (the federal government is run by the other political party), but the other news channel says the store closure decisions are made locally. I'm confused!"

Trust in the government diminishes if the government continues to worry the population about dire events that don't materialize, such as global cooling or a massive spike in terrorist attacks on American soil, or if it contradicts itself over and over. The government then needs to create new ways to instill fear into people so that they can continue to captivate the public's attention.

"In the COVID-19 pandemic, for example, when a few people die in a city of millions—which is, of course a tragedy,—major networks' coverage could lead one to perceive the whole city is unsafe."[44] This led to fear and panic, which caused the government to shut the doors of businesses across the city. This cascaded across the state, to other states, the country, and the world.

Obviously, we needed to take this drastic precaution at the onset due to the fact that we didn't know what we were dealing with. But as time went on, people became skeptical as the percentage of deaths first predicted was much higher than the actual data.

How to Deal with Fear of Government

Beware of What Government Thinks is "Good" For You

I'm a law-abiding citizen, and if the government tells me to do or not do something under penalty of arrest, I'll comply (temporarily, then I'll find a new government). But you should not settle for what is mandated and accept it as the final answer to whatever "problem" the government is trying to address. Take a look at it and see if it makes logical sense or if it's good for you in the long term.

Take a look at the government and those who run it. What kind of laws or suggestions are being implemented, and what results do you think the government is aiming to achieve? Is it something you disagree with? Contact your local representative and voice your opinion. If nothing happens, get support together and vote them out! Hey, you can even consider a run for the position if you're passionate about the issue.

The point is that politicians and parties are put in power by the people they represent. It's important that the politicians don't become complacent and are held accountable if they're voted in because of their beliefs and what they plan to accomplish. Be wary of career politicians who just want a job and really haven't done anything to improve your community or way of life.

Analyze All Information Available Before You Vote

Some individuals are loyal to one political party and will vote for whoever runs under the party ticket. They go into the voting booth and vote that party all the way down the column. Here are three things you should consider:

1. Assess why you want to vote the way you do. Is it due to a historical pattern of voting instilled in you by others? If you vote a certain way, does it directly impact you and your situation? What is the track record of that party in your area? Have things gotten better, worse, or stayed the same since they were in power?

2. If there is a current situation that is negatively affecting you and your loved ones (such as the pandemic or economic strife), how did it arise, and how are your elected officials dealing with it? Are their actions helping or hurting the situation? Have you analyzed a majority—if not all—of the actual data available to determine how it affects your vote?

3. Regarding individual candidates: Do they have a track record of actually getting things

done? Is the candidate a competent individual, or are they just the official candidate because it is their "time" to run for office?

In short, take a step back, ask some questions, and analyze the data. As Ross Perot put it when he ran for president: "Vote Your Conscience!"

10

Fear of Healthcare

"I mean some doctor told me I had six
months to live and I went to their funeral."

—Keith Richards

We all want to be healthy and live a long and happy life. The medical profession understands this and is committed to helping everyone live as long as they can to enjoy their families and contribute to society. In general, we visit doctors annually for our physicals, and usually, we're given a clean bill of health.

However, sometimes we're diagnosed with elevated cholesterol or blood pressure and are prescribed medications to help "solve" this problem so we can live a "normal" life. It seems like taking a pill is an easy solution to fix the problem. So, unfortunately, that's what many people do. But are we really addressing the cause of the issues? Could our problem actually be a poor diet? Could it be increased stress levels from a job we don't enjoy?

Direct-to-Consumer Advertising (DTCA) for pharmaceuticals was legalized in the U.S. in 1997. In the *Forbes* article, "Are Direct-To-Consumer Ads For Drugs Doing More Harm than Good?" Reenita Das writes:

> "While DTCA has some positive effects, these commercials tend to mislead patients and can result in the breakdown of the doctor-patient relationship. The pros of DCTA were primarily based on the belief that, when patients saw ads for drugs that aligned with their symptoms, they would start a dialogue with their physician and take a more active role in their healthcare journey. The cons are the depiction of a 'wonder drug' that claims to offer a cure and help patients live long and healthy lives. This advertising appeals to individuals who fear the ailment or disease they have, and it creates a situation where the patient becomes the doctor—demanding that the medication be immediately prescribed.[45]

Marie is a stay-at-home mom to two great kids, and her husband works to support the family. She wanted to make some extra money, so she started a business on the side. But it didn't generate sales, so she stopped doing the work. She started feeling down and had a hard time starting and moving through her day. One day, she saw an ad with a woman who initially looked sad as she folded laundry. Then, in the next scene, she was out with her friends, laughing and enjoying dinner.

The word "Solarexo" flashed on the screen and piqued Marie's interest. In the ad's final scene, the woman smiled and laughed with her kids as she folded laundry.

Marie decided then and there to ask her doctor about Solarexo. She was swayed by a commercial that peddled prescriptions to solve a problem. In the end, Marie feared staying in the same depressed situation because she was missing so much more in life. This forced her to act and call her doctor to demand this medication.

Marie's situation is a perfect example of how pharmaceutical and medical-treatment commercials affect society. These types of commercials are very effective because they offer a quick and easy solution to people's problems. They also generate a significant amount of revenue for the healthcare industry.

The article, "Do not get sold on drug advertising," by *Harvard Health Publishing*, presents some interesting facts about drug advertisements:

- The United States and New Zealand are the only countries where drug makers are allowed to market prescription drugs directly to consumers.

- Drug-specific ads fall into two main categories: product claim and reminder.

  - A product claim ad names a drug, notes its generic name and the condition it treats, and talks about both benefits and risks in a balanced fashion. (It's common for any potential side effects to be described rapidly at the end or written in small type that makes it hard to read and comprehend.)

- A reminder ad gives the drug's name, but not the drug's use. The assumption is that the audience already knows what the drug is for. This kind of ad does not contain risk information because it does not discuss the condition the drug treats or how well it works.

- The FDA does not approve prescription drug ads in advance, but its staff tries to monitor them to ensure claims are not false or misleading.

- Prescription drugs accounted for nearly 17 percent of total healthcare spending in 2015, up from about 7 percent in the 1990s before the revised FDA guidelines went into effect.[46]

Another big fear that people have with healthcare is having unexpected medical bills, particularly as standardized pricing makes it almost impossible for patients to get an accurate estimate of healthcare costs beforehand.

According to a recent poll discussed in the article, "Fear in Healthcare," 67 percent of people worry more about unexpected medical bills than they do insurance deductibles, prescription drug costs, rent, food, and gas.[47]

Mental illness is a serious (and growing) problem, too. In the same article, the author writes: "One fear that is shared by patients AND clinicians is the fear of being shunned and stigmatized if they admit to having mental health or addiction issues. As a result, many suffer in silence."[48]

The desire to avoid public stigma causes individuals to drop out of treatment or avoid it entirely for fear of being associated with negative stereotypes. Public stigma may also influence the beliefs and behaviors of those closest to individuals with mental illness, including friends, family, and employers.[49]

How to Deal with Fear of Healthcare

Don't Take That Pill Yet!

If we don't feel well or are depressed, it's easy for us to call a doctor and get a prescription. We fill it at the local pharmacy and everything is okay. However, have we really looked at the root cause of the problem we're experiencing?

Use the "Five Why" approach: Keep asking "Why?" to get to the root cause of the problem and determine why you feel the way you feel. Question if you *really* need a particular medication. Don't play doctor and give yourself a diagnosis, and understand that a lot of the medications manufactured today usually have side effects attached to them. This could mean that you need another pill to take care of the side effect from the first pill!

Here are some ideas to try before you pop that pill:

- Talk to someone about the issues you're facing: your spouse, a friend, or a therapist. You have to let people know how you're feeling, especially if you think they're contributing to your problem.

- Make taking care of yourself your first priority. If you aren't thinking clearly, you can't help others. Start a routine every day that includes some type of meditation—I like guided meditation. Also, get on a daily program to move your body. Even a brisk walk every day can help. After a while, you'll feel like a new person and you can possibly avoid that medication altogether.

- ◆ Eat right. Recent studies show that there is a direct connection between your microbiome—your gut—and your brain. The phrase, "You are what you eat," is true! What we eat directly affects our moods and our bodily functions. Daily consumption of alcohol can also have a detrimental effect on our overall being. Eat clean. For example, eat raw vegetables and lean meats like chicken and fish. For dessert, grab an apple instead of that piece of chocolate cake. You'll feel a lot better!

- ◆ Holistic alternatives. If I'm in a hospital and the nurse says to me, "Take this pill or you will die," I'll take the pill. But if you're presented with an option to take a pill for back pain or go for acupuncture, try the needles first and see what happens. What do you have to lose? There are also a lot of daily natural supplements you can take to help your body stay healthy. Who wants manufactured chemicals coursing through their veins when there might be other natural and less invasive options?

Get Some Form of Health Insurance

Health insurance, especially in the U.S., is expensive. However, it's worth it to alleviate the stress caused by not knowing how you are going to pay for your next medical bill. The prices of prescription drugs are through the roof, and though name-brand drugs are expensive, there is often a generic substitute that is less so, and that's covered by insurance. If you can't afford typical insurance, check out Healthcare.gov to see what programs they offer.

11

Conclusion

"The only thing we have to Fear, is Fear itself."

—Franklin D. Roosevelt

Fear can arise in all sorts of different situations. How you deal with that fear will shape the course of your life and the lives of those around you.

You must determine whether your fear is real or something that you've fabricated based on past events or potential outcomes. If the fear is real and imminent—like an angry animal or someone threatening you or your family—you should obviously act fast. But if the fear is a thought that fuels an emotion, pause and consider the thought for a moment. What is the actual likelihood of something bad or life-threatening happening to you? If you are using past events to form a conclusion on what will happen in the future, stop! Keep the past in the past where it belongs. If you're struggling with fear, get the help you need. Talk to a friend or seek some guidance from a professional. There are a lot of people out there who want to see you win!

It's your life, your decision, your destiny. Now get out there and Crush That Fear!

12

16 Techniques to Crush Your Fear

> "Our fears are more numerous than our dangers, and we suffer more in our imagination than reality."
> —Seneca

1. Don't let family members derail you from achieving your dreams. Consider the source of "advice" and their experience in the areas in which you want to excel.

2. Limit your time with family members who don't support your ideas and dreams.

3. If you have an idea for a new direction in life or a new business, make sure your significant other is on board and supportive. Make them a part of your dream.

4. Acknowledge your strengths and ideas and come up with a plan to capitalize on them.

5. If you have an idea, limit your analysis before

putting your plan into action. You need to test your idea to determine if it will be successful.

6. Remember: Fear exists in the past or the future, don't bring it into the present.

7. Consider your family's well-being and important events *before* workplace demands (unless you will be terminated for failing to accomplish a workplace task).

8. If workplace demands cause you to compromise your integrity, start looking for another job.

9. You should be able to trust your partner and friends. Have honest conversations with them if you are uneasy about something.

10. Don't be overprotective of your kids; they need to fail at some things to learn.

11. Be yourself in social media posts.

12. Limit your time on social media by tracking how much actual time you spend there and adjusting accordingly.

13. Understand that the media is primarily fear-based and wants to get you to look at their ads.

14. Keep on top of how your kids are performing in school and structure a program of encouragement rather than demand that they get excellent scores across the board.

15. Do the research on candidates before you elect them to office. Find out what facts are real and dismiss the rest.

16. Ask your doctor if there is an alternative to taking a pill to solve a problem.

Acknowledgments

I am indebted to my daughters, Sophia, Olivia, and Valentina, for their love, support, and encouragement to face my fears and be the best dad I can be. They are my "Why."

Special thanks to Lisa Akoury-Ross, owner of SDP Publishing Solutions, LLC, for her guidance and encouragement. Also, editors Katie Barger and Robert Astle who challenged and advised me to write my best.

Friends who offered advice and support include Stacy Raske and amazing humans in Apex and Arete.

Finally, I'd like to acknowledge my mom and dad, who wanted me to be the best I could possibly be.

About the Author

MICHAEL POWER is a CPA, author, speaker, entrepreneur, and father of three beautiful girls who has started multiple revenue-generating companies both in the U.S. and Europe. He currently hosts the Crushing Your Fear podcast and has learned to conquer fear through examining it, learning from it, leaving the past behind, and adopting gratitude and a positive outlook for the future.

END NOTES

1. "Understanding the Stress Response," accessed April 23, 2022, https://www.health.harvard.edu/staying-healthy/understanding-the-stress-response.

2. "A Brief History of Anxiety & Fear," accessed April 23, 2022, https://explorable.com/e/history-of-anxiety-and-fear.

3. "A Brief History of Anxiety & Fear."

4. "A Brief History of Anxiety & Fear."

5. "A Brief History of Anxiety & Fear."

6. "A Brief History of Anxiety & Fear."

7. "A Brief History of Anxiety & Fear."

8. "Fears, Outbreaks, and Pandemics: Lessons Learned," accessed April 23, 2022, https://www.psychiatrictimes.com/view/fears-out-breaks-and-pandemics-lessons-learned.

9. "Why Are Americans Still so Afraid of Islamist Terrorism?" – The Washington Post," accessed April 23, 2022, https://www.washing-tonpost.com/news/monkey-cage/wp/2018/03/23/why-are-ameri-cans-still-so-afraid-of-islamic-terrorism/.

10. "Why Are Americans Still so Afraid of Islamist Terrorism?"

11. "Atychiphobia: Understanding Fear of Failure," accessed April 23, 2022, https://www.healthline.com/health/atychiphobia#outlook.

12. "Atychiphobia: Understanding Fear of Failure."

13. "Atychiphobia: Understanding Fear of Failure."

14. "How to Overcome Your Fear of Failure," accessed April 23, 2022, https://hbr.org/2018/12/how-to-overcome-your-fear-of-failure.

15. "How to Overcome Your Biggest Workplace Fears," accessed April 23, 2022, https://www.fastcompany.com/3046817/how-to-over-come-your-biggest-workplace-fears.

16. "Fear of Public Speaking: How Can I Overcome It?" – Mayo Clin-ic," accessed April 23, 2022, https://www.mayoclinic.org/diseases-conditions/specific-phobias/expert-answers/fear-of-public-speaking/faq-20058416.

17. "3 Relationship Fears Literally Every Person Has, Because You're Not Alone," Elite Daily, accessed April 23, 2022, https://www.

elitedaily.com/p/3-normal-fears-in-relationships-that-basically-everybody-has-so-dont-worry-8310419.

18. "3 Relationship Fears Literally Every Person Has, Because You're Not Alone."

19. "The Many Shades of Fear-Based Parenting | Psychology Today," accessed April 23, 2022, https://www.psychologytoday.com/us/blog/freedom-learn/201903/the-many-shades-fear-based-parenting

20. "The Many Shades of Fear-Based Parenting | Psychology Today."

21. "The Many Shades of Fear-Based Parenting | Psychology Today."

22. "Hollywood Celebrities Show the Way to Bribe Your Kid into College," CCN.com, March 13, 2019, https://www.ccn.com/hollywood-celebrities-show-the-way-to-bribe-your-kid-into-college/.

23. "The Many Shades of Fear-Based Parenting | Psychology Today."

24. "Shakespeare," William, *Hamlet*, n.d.

25. "Dopamine, Smartphones & You: A Battle for Your Time," *Science in the News* (blog), May 1, 2018, https://sitn.hms.harvard.edu/flash/2018/dopamine-smartphones-battle-time/.

26. "Dopamine, Smartphones & You."

27. "Dopamine, Smartphones & You."

28. "Social Media Addiction," Addiction Center, accessed April 23, 2022, https://www.addictioncenter.com/drugs/social-media-addiction/.

29. "Social Media Addiction."

30. "Social Media Addiction."

31. "5 Real Social Media Fears and How to Overcome Them," Kruse Control Inc, June 8, 2021, https://www.krusecontrolinc.com/social-media-fears-how-to-overcome/.

32. "If It Bleeds, It Leads: Understanding Fear-Based Media | Psychology Today," accessed April 23, 2022, https://www.psychologytoday.com/us/blog/two-takes-depression/201106/if-it-bleeds-it-leads-understanding-fear-based-media.

33. "If It Bleeds, It Leads."

34. "Mass Media, Crime, and the Discourse of Fear," The Hedgehog Review, accessed April 23, 2022, https://hedgehogreview.com/issues/fear-itself/articles/mass-media-crime-and-the-discourse-of-fear.

35. "Mass Media, Crime, and the Discourse of Fear."

36. "If It Bleeds, It Leads."

37. LaRae Quy, "How to Overcome The Power Of Fear-Based Media,"

Advisorpedia, accessed April 23, 2022, https://www.advisorpedia. com/growth/how-to-overcome-the-power-of-fear-based-media/.

38. "If It Bleeds, It Leads."

39. "Helping Students Overcome Their Fear of Failure," EAIE, May 30, 2013, https://www.eaie.org/blog/helping-students-overcome-fear-of-failure.html.

40. "Helping Students Overcome Their Fear of Failure."

41. "Opinion: A Neuroscientist Explains How Politicians and the Media Use Fear to Make Us Hate without Thinking – MarketWatch," accessed April 23, 2022, https://www.marketwatch.com/story/a-neuroscientist-explains-how-politicians-and-the-media-use-fear-to-make-us-hate-without-thinking-2019-07-18.

42. "Opinion: A Neuroscientist Explains How Politicians and the Media Use Fear to Make Us Hate without Thinking – MarketWatch.

43. On The Coast × CBC News ×, "Fear in Politics Goes Back to Ancient Times: Here Are 5 Examples | CBC News, "CBC, October 2, 2015, https://www.cbc.ca/news/canada/british-columbia/fear-in-politics-5-examples-through-history-1.3251520.

44. "Opinion: A Neuroscientist Explains How Politicians and the Media Use Fear to Make Us Hate without Thinking – MarketWatch.

45. "Are Direct-To-Consumer Ads For Drugs Doing More Harm than Good?," accessed April 23, 2022, https://www.forbes.com/sites/reenitadas/2019/05/14/direct-to-consumer-drug-ads-are-they-doing-more-harm-than-good/?sh=57f3744f4dfc.

46. "Do Not Get Sold on Drug Advertising," Harvard Health, February 14, 2017, https://www.health.harvard.edu/medications/do-not-get-sold-on-drug-advertising.

47. "Fear in Healthcare," *Hcldr* (blog), October 29, 2018, https://hcldr. wordpress.com/2018/10/28/fear-in-healthcare/.

48. "Fear in Healthcare."

49. "Fear in Healthcare."

BIBLIOGRAPHY

Elite Daily. "3 Relationship Fears Literally Every Person Has, Because You're Not Alone." Accessed April 23, 2022. https://www.elitedaily.com/p/3-normal-fears-in-relationships-that-basically-everybody-has-so-dont-worry-8310419.

Kruse Control Inc. "5 Real Social Media Fears and How to Overcome Them," June 8, 2021. https://www.krusecontrolinc.com/social-media-fears-how-to-overcome/.

"A Brief History of Anxiety & Fear." Accessed April 23, 2022. https://explorable.com/e/history-of-anxiety-and-fear.

"Are Direct-To-Consumer Ads For Drugs Doing More Harm than Good?" Accessed April 23, 2022. https://www.forbes.com/sites/reenitadas/2019/05/14/direct-to-consumer-drug-ads-are-they-doing-more-harm-than-good/?sh=57f3744f4dfc.

"Atychiphobia: Understanding Fear of Failure." Accessed April 23, 2022. https://www.healthline.com/health/atychiphobia#outlook.

Harvard Health. "Do Not Get Sold on Drug Advertising," February 14, 2017. https://www.health.harvard.edu/medications/do-not-get-sold-on-drug-advertising.

Science in the News. "Dopamine, Smartphones & You: A Battle for Your Time," May 1, 2018. https://sitn.hms.harvard.edu/flash/2018/dopamine-smartphones-battle-time/.

hcldr. "Fear in Healthcare," October 29, 2018. https://hcldr.wordpress.com/2018/10/28/fear-in-healthcare/.

"Fear of Public Speaking: How Can I Overcome It? - Mayo Clinic." Accessed April 23, 2022. https://www.mayoclinic.org/diseases-conditions/specific-phobias/expert-answers/fear-of-public-speaking/faq-20058416.

"Fears, Outbreaks, and Pandemics: Lessons Learned." Accessed April 23, 2022. https://www.psychiatrictimes.com/view/fears-outbreaks-and-pandemics-lessons-learned.

EAIE. "Helping Students Overcome Their Fear of Failure," May 30, 2013. https://www.eaie.org/blog/helping-students-overcome-fear-of-failure.html.

CCN.com. "Hollywood Celebrities Show the Way to Bribe Your Kid into College," March 13, 2019. https://www.ccn.com/hollywood-celebrities-show-the-way-to-bribe-your-kid-into-college/.

"How to Overcome Your Biggest Workplace Fears." Accessed April 23, 2022. https://www.fastcompany.com/3046817/how-to-overcome-your-biggest-workplace-fears.

"How to Overcome Your Fear of Failure." Accessed April 23, 2022. https://hbr.org/2018/12/how-to-overcome-your-fear-of-failure.

"If It Bleeds, It Leads: Understanding Fear-Based Media | Psychology Today." Accessed April 23, 2022. https://www.psychologytoday.com/us/blog/two-takes-depression/201106/if-it-bleeds-it-leads-understanding-fear-based-media.

The Hedgehog Review. "Mass Media, Crime, and the Discourse of Fear." Accessed April 23, 2022. https://hedgehogreview.com/issues/fear-itself/articles/mass-media-crime-and-the-discourse-of-fear.

News ·, On The Coast · CBC. "Fear in Politics Goes Back to Ancient Times: Here Are 5 Examples | CBC News." CBC, October 2, 2015. https://www.cbc.ca/news/canada/british-columbia/fear-in-politics-5-examples-through-history-1.3251520.

"Opinion: A Neuroscientist Explains How Politicians and the Media Use Fear to Make Us Hate without Thinking - MarketWatch." Accessed April 23, 2022. https://www.marketwatch.com/story/a-neuroscientist-explains-how-politicians-and-the-media-use-fear-to-make-us-hate-without-thinking-2019-07-18.

Quy, LaRae. "How To Overcome The Power Of Fear-Based Media." Advisorpedia. Accessed April 23, 2022. https://www.advisorpedia.com/growth/how-to-overcome-the-power-of-fear-based-media/.

Shakespeare, William. *Hamlet*, n.d.

Addiction Center. "Social Media Addiction." Accessed April 23, 2022. https://www.addictioncenter.com/drugs/social-media-addiction/.

"The Many Shades of Fear-Based Parenting | Psychology Today." Accessed April 23, 2022. https://www.psychologytoday.com/us/blog/freedom-learn/201903/the-many-shades-fear-based-parenting.

"Understanding the Stress Response." | Harvard Health Publishing, July 6, 2020. https://www.health.harvard.edu/staying-healthy/understanding-the-stress-response.

"Why Are Americans Still so Afraid of Islamist Terrorism?" - The Washington Post. Accessed April 23, 2022. https://www.washingtonpost.com/news/monkey-cage/wp/2018/03/23/why-are-americans-still-so-afraid-of-islamic-terrorism/.

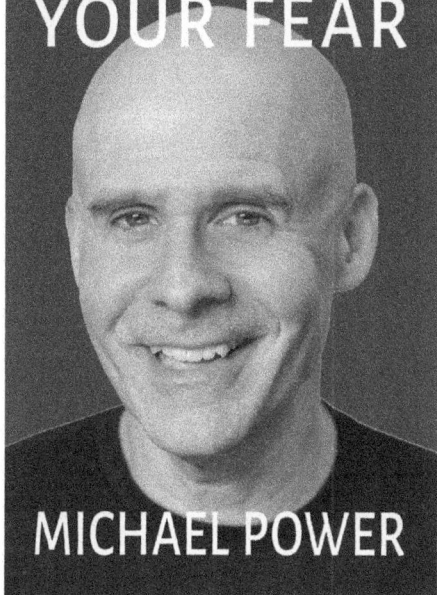

Crushing Your Fear

Michael Power

https://www.crushingyourfear.com/

Available through:
Ingram
Amazon
BN.com
SDPPublishing.com

 SDP Publishing

Contact us at: info@SDPPublishing.com